Violence in Ireland

veritas

Violence in Ireland
and Christian Conscience

From addresses given by *Cahal B. Daly*
Bishop of Ardagh and Clonmacnois

Veritas Publications, Dublin 1973

First published 1973 by
Veritas Publications, Pranstown House,
Booterstown Avenue, Co. Dublin.

A division of
The Catholic Communications
Institute of Ireland.

Cover designed by Steven Hope.
Typographical layout by Liam Miller.
Printed in Ireland by
Beacon Printing Company Limited.

ISBN 0-901810-61-4.

OCLC: 28111752

Contents

To the memory of
Father Hugh Mullan (†9th August 1972)
and
Father Noel Fitzpatrick († 9th July 1972)
victims of street violence
who offered their lives with Christ
that men might be freed from hate
and died speaking forgiveness and praying for
reconciliation trying by their deaths
to show us a better way.

Foreword

Church leaders are often urged and rightly urged nowadays to speak with a prophetic voice. Sometimes, unfortunately, this seems to amount to a call to take sides passionately, to commit oneself with at least emotional violence, to abound in the rhetoric of moral denunciation.

But the biblical prophet does not take sides — except for God. The biblical prophet is the man who, appointed and inspired by God, interprets contemporary events in the chosen people's history in the light of God's law and covenant.

The prophet in the New Testament dispensation has the same role; but it is now governed by the nature of the new law and the new covenant brought into the world by Christ. The new law is the law of love of the neighbour, any neighbour, as son of the same Father, as blood brother in the blood of Christ. The new covenant is the covenant of God's love for all men without exclusion or distinction, sealed in the blood of Christ, shed for us and also for all other men without exception.

It is the covenant committing us to that totally self-giving love which was shown in Christ's body wholly given to us, totally given up for us. There is no truly prophetic voice, since Christ, which does not speak of love and speak in love. No word which insults or divides can be the word of a Christian prophet; but only the word which heals and reconciles.

The prophet must speak the truth; but he speaks it in love and in conscious and deliberate effort and desire to be just to both sides, and so to be listened to on both sides of the relevant divisions. He will not expect complete approbation from either side. If he received unqualified consent from either side, this would be an almost certain sign of failure in fairness to the other.

The following addresses claim no sort of prophetic charism. They were motivated by a sense of obligation to try and face the judgement of God which the Christian must see in this, one of the gravest crises ever to have overtaken Christianity in Ireland. They arose out of a sense of duty to try to interpret tragic contemporary events in Ireland in the light of Christ's law of love; to try to find some way through the shambles of destruction to the peace of Christ.

They are reprinted now out of the same sense of duty, in the same sincere desire to prepare some way for Christ to come and speak to our desperate situation and be listened to and obeyed when he speaks. The author's only wish would be that some remark somewhere in what follows might help someone to think through and live through this desperate situation without compromising his Christian faith and hope; might help someone to pray more insistently, to long more intensely, to work more courageously, for peace in our land; might help to guide someone's feet into the way of Christ's peace, now in 1973.

✠ Cahal B. Daly
Bishop of Ardagh and Clonmacnois

23rd March, 1973

Part One

Our Present Distress

Violence is brutal and brutalising. It injures those who inflict it as much as those on whom it is inflicted. Above all it injures the innocent — the old and the ill, the expectant mothers, the mothers of large young families. It injures the children and youth. Members of a whole generation of Irish people in the North are put in danger of being permanently injured, emotionally and morally, by the present scourge of violence.

Chaos or Community?

From an address in Mohill, Co. Leitrim, organised by The Leitrim Guardian and Mohill Motivation and Community Cooperation, on Sunday, December 12th, 1971.

The bishops have again and again in the most solemn words condemned violence as unjustified and evil. The evidence mounts, as news bulletin follows news bulletin, that the tree of violence is evil and that its fruits become more and more ruthlessly evil with every bomb and every cold-blooded murder.

But the bishops have no less courageously condemned the brutalities and inhumanities of the other violence which is military repression. And the bishops have not ceased to declare that the basic injustice, which the long-standing denial of political and social equality in the North represents, must be tackled boldly at its root.

This problem is by far the gravest issue in British and Irish politics at the present time. It would be unforgiveable that politicians, whether in Britain or in Ireland, should let cowardice or weakness, inertia or party interest take precedence over human lives and the welfare and future of entire communities. History will judge very severely those who fail to match the gravity of the present situation with the wisdom and the courage of their political initiatives.

Martin Luther King, who died in 1968 as a martyr of non-violence, had written before his death a book, posthumously published, with the title *Chaos or Community?* That is the stark alternative facing the North of Ireland at the present time. Unless we build a community, based upon social justice and full equality of political participation, the result can only be chaos and the utter social and economic disintegration of civilised society. We must pray that the responsible leaders may prove worthy in this hour of crisis.

The Lesson of Derry's Dead

Sermon at a Mass for the victims of "Bloody Sunday" in Derry, celebrated in St. Mel's Cathedral, Longford, on February 2nd, 1972.

Few events in fifty years have so shocked and horrified the Irish nation, so aroused and so united the Irish people, as the awful killings in Derry on last Sunday. It would be irresponsibility, bordering on madness, for anyone, but especially for the British Government, to underestimate the depth and the danger of the emotion gripping this country at this time.

But we are gathered for prayer, not for bitterness. Talk of vengeance, retaliation, reprisals, can have no place in a Christian community. The very word "retaliation" comes from a primitive and barbarous age, which practised the *lex talionis*, the law which demanded "an eye for an eye". This law features still in the Old Testament. What is usually not realised, however, is that already here there is a beginning of a taming of this wild code. What it means in the Old Testament really is : "Only an eye for an eye" — punishment, in other words, must be proportioned to the crime.

But this rough justice of the Old Law is totally superseded by Christ's law of love, which is the New Law. Here, in this Cathedral, before the altar of the greatest love the world has ever known, in the presence of the silent, innocent, non-violent Victim of the world's violence and sin, no words are permitted to a Christian people but the words of Christ: "Father, forgive them; they do not know what they are doing." (*Luke* 23:34.)

In this holy place, in the presence of the Lamb of God, living in the Eucharist to make uninterrupted intercession for the guilty world, what voice can we listen to but his, who said: "You have learnt how it was said: eye for eye and tooth for tooth . . . But I say this to you: love your enemies and pray for those who persecute you; in this way you will be sons of your Father in heaven." (*Matthew* 5:38-44.)

To whom can we turn for guidance in this dark hour, except to him to whom Peter said, on the day he promised us this holy Eucharist: "Lord, to whom shall we go? You have the message of eternal life, and we believe, we know, that you are the Holy One of God." (*John* 6:67-9.)

PRAYER

Our first response, therefore, to this tragedy is prayer. Firstly, prayer to the Lord of Mercy to take the souls of these innocent victims straight to his presence, to "stand for ever in front of his throne and serve him day and night in his sanctuary . . . where God will wipe away all tears from their eyes" (*Revelation* 7:15-17), and give them a peace they did not find in this world, a peace this world, even at its best, can never give.

Secondly, prayer for the bereaved, that the "gentle Father and the God of all consolation may comfort them in all their sorrows" now and in the saddened years before them; prayer that "as the sufferings of Christ overflow to us, so, through Christ, our consolation too may overflow." (*Corinthians* 1:3-4.)

We shall pray too that God may take bitterness out of their hearts and preserve them from the spirit of revenge and hate. For we remember that when two disciples once wanted to have a village burnt out in reprisal for their hostility to our Lord, he replied "You do not know of what spirit you are." (*Luke* 9 :55.) We do not forget that one of these two fire-bombing disciples was later to be the greatest teacher of Jesus' love, John, the disciple who to the end of an unusually long life had only one sermon, endlessly repeated : "My little children, love one another." And when people grew bored and said : "Not that . . . again"; or when they grumbled and protested : "How can he, how dare he, command us to love these evil Roman oppressors?", John's answer always was : "But this is all the Master taught; and he left us no other law."

We pray too for all those, now counted by hundreds, not tens, who have lost their lives since these black days began in the North with the terrible events of August, 1969. We pray for all alike, Protestant and Catholic, British as well as Irish, for "All alike have sinned and fallen short of the glory of God" (*Romans* 3 :23) and need his redeeming mercy.

We pray that their deaths may be accepted by the Lord in expiation for all the wrongs Ireland has suffered and all the evil Irishmen have done, and in atonement for all the hatred this island has known; and that their blood may be used by God to purge the bitterness out of all Irish hearts and teach us at least to live together like Christians and love one another like the brothers we are, in Christ.

We pray finally, in the words of O'Casey's Mrs Boyle, spoken on the occasion of a tragedy just such as Sunday's :

Sacred Heart of Jesus,
take away our hearts of stone
and give us hearts of flesh.

Take away this murdherin' hate
and give us thine own eternal love.

THE FUTURE

We do not forget today that the future Ireland is one
in which we must and will find a place, in equal enjoyment of human rights and freedom, for a million
Northern Protestants. Nothing we think or say in these
days of grief and frustration must be allowed to damage
the prospect of that future Ireland. For there are two
traditions in this island and not one only, two historical
and cultural ways of remembering, reacting and thinking, two religious traditions, two distinct ways of being
Irish. They are distinct but need not and must not be
hostile; for both are ways of being Irish.

If present hatreds continue in the North the two
traditions can only destroy one another by each first
destroying itself. In reconciliation and collaboration,
we can together build an Ireland in which all Irishmen
can be proud to live. In mutual hostility and violence,
we will succeed only in making an Ireland in which
no Irishman would wish to live and which no foreigner
would wish to visit.

BRITAIN'S RESPONSIBILITY

Many of us had hoped that Britain might, in this post-
colonial age, at last attempt to atone for centuries of
harm and hurt in her relations with Ireland by provid-
ing the firm and decisive leadership needed to guarantee
justice in the North and build a future in peace for the
whole of Ireland. These hopes have up to now been
cruelly disappointed. This time of Ireland's greatest
need has also been the time of Britain's most miserable
desertion.

The British Government has failed in the most elementary responsibility of a government — it has not governed. It has not led; but has let itself be misled, misinformed, misused. It has betrayed the Irish people.

But it has also betrayed the British people, by making them accessories to a policy which flaunts all British standards of decency and justice, and by letting their Army be committed to behaviour of which British people should be ashamed and by which British people are being disgraced in the eyes of the world.

Britain's leaders were warned again and again of the gravity of the situation existing in the North of Ireland and of the increasingly dangerous state of emotion and feeling in the rest of Ireland. They were warned of the grave and urgent need for resolute political action, for radical structural reforms. They did not listen. Will they listen now? Will they ever learn to take Irishmen seriously? Must there be tragedy piled upon Derry's tragedy before Britain's leaders learn that there is not a military solution, that there is now no alternative to a radical new deal for all Ireland?

Britain, through its present policies, has let itself become totally alienated from the minority in the North of Ireland. They have sought their information about that minority from the Stormont Government. But Stormont has not ever spoken for the Catholic minority; it has never spoken to that Catholic minority. Above all, in the last two years it has ceased even to try to speak to that minority; it can now never hope to speak for them again.

But fifty years of failure by some Irishmen need not mean a future of despair for all this island. There is enough justice, integrity and moral courage in the British people and in many British politicians to ensure that they will not indefinitely tolerate what is now being done in their name. There is enough justice, integrity and decency among Northern Protestants to bring them to recognise the failures and admit the faults of the past and embolden them to build a future not for themselves only but for the minority in their midst, and not *for* that minority only but *with* it, and therefore with the rest of Ireland to which that minority irrevocably belongs. There is enough insight, realism and courage among Northern Protestants to justify the hope that they too will see that their future lies not over their Catholic neighbours but with them, not against the rest of Ireland but with it.

The gifts of Northern Protestants — gifts of intelligence, skill and industry; of honesty, decency, Christian charity and generosity — have been used to create institutions and structures of education, culture, health, social welfare, which we in the rest of Ireland could envy and should try to emulate. It is part of the North's tragedy that all this was an attempt to build a noble superstructure upon a political substructure which was radically and irremediably defective.

No society can ultimately be better than its politics. This is why all Christians must now learn that an absolutely primary field for Christian action and concern is precisely politics. Politics is too important to be left to demagogues. It is forty years since Maritain called for saints of politics. If the concept seems strange, this is only because we have got strange ideas of sanctity and very diminished notions of Christianity. When Northern Protestants begin to channel into politics the human virtues which have ennobled their tradition and the Christian faith which is their most valued heritage, then a new future can dawn for all of Ireland.

HOPE

So, even in these days of gloom and grief, the last word for the Christian is one of hope. For death is not the end. It was not the end for Christ, though his death had all the marks of disgrace and failure and defeat. But the darkness of Good Friday was only prelude to an Easter dawn that knows no setting, the dawn of a light which history's darkness can never again extinguish.

In Ireland long ago they called Christ the King of Friday. His men they called Friday's men — the poor, the despised, the defeated. But he is the King of Friday's men; and in his Sunday victory the dead rise and the defeated triumph, and he becomes the King of Sunday's men. In him we can all be Sunday's men, men of the Resurrection, men of indestructible hope.

The Aldershot Explosion

From an address at the opening of a Macra na Feirme Seminar on Development in Longford, on February 22nd, 1972.

As one who has on many occasions in the past condemned British atrocities in the North of Ireland, I find myself with the sad duty on this occasion of condemning an Irish atrocity. I take this opportunity of condemning in the strongest possible terms the barbaric explosion which was perpetrated today at Aldershot. This is a wicked deed and deprives its authors for all time of the moral right to condemn atrocities by the British.

This evil thing could be authorised, planned and executed and can now be approved only by men who have let their minds be perverted and their consciences corrupted by an evil philosophy. For it is a barbaric code which holds that innocent lives can be taken to avenge life and it is an unChristian and radically evil principle to say that the end justifies the means. This indeed is the most immoral of all immoral principles. Indeed it is the root of all immorality. This was the source of all the crimes of history from Nero to Stalin and from Cromwell to Hitler.

May this horrible crime at least have one good effect, of bringing about a final repudiation by all our people of such evil means. May the prayers of the thirteen innocent dead of Derry, whose names were indecently invoked to justify this deed, obtain repentance and for-giveness for those guilty of it. May the prayers of the Derry dead and those of the Aldershot dead and of all the other Irish and British, Protestant and Catholic dead who have died in the last three tragic years, now obtain God's mercy for us all and bring peace at last — peace with justice, peace with tolerance and reconcilia-tion, to all in this tortured land of ours.

Part Two

Violence or Non-Violence?

A Christian is not obliged to hold that recourse to violence is in all circumstances and of necessity wrong. But grave indeed are the consequences of violence and heavy is the responsibility of those who resort to it.

Violence or Non-Violence?

The text of an address delivered in Longford on World Peace Day, January 1st, 1972. The address was published in The Furrow *(February, 1972) and is reprinted here by kind permission of the Editor.*

THE DEMYTHOLOGISING OF WAR

There has been growing strongly in recent years in nearly all countries an emotional and moral revulsion from war as an irrational, barbarous and evil thing. It is being made increasingly difficult for militarists to propagate the myth of the glory and glamour of war. War is undergoing a process of radical "demythologising". A myth that has exercised a fatal fascination over men's minds all through human history seems at last to be capable of being deprived of all rational credibility and of much of its persuasive power. The propagandist visor of the war-god is being torn off and the face of the moronic blonde beast of war revealed.

Many factors have converged to bring about this result. Television has brought the gory horror of war right into the homes of combatant nations. The immediate vision of the blood and the pain, the brutal atrocity, the senseless destruction, have made the militaristic slogans sound offensive, the propaganda posters seem obscene.

Literature, drama, art, objective historical research, have all made their distinctive contribution. A tide of pacifism seems to be rising everywhere which is based on reasoned assessment of experience and on a calm determination to free man from myths. This could perhaps be seen as part of man's progress to maturity, part of the emergence of "man come of age".

THE MORALITY OF WAR

Literature, art and journalism have a powerful influence upon our moral insights and judgements. Moral progress can be stimulated by an enlargement of experience and imagination, such as is effected by creative and morally perceptive writers, artists and media-communicators. The opposite, of course, is also true; and conscience can be coarsened by writers and journalists who subordinate moral principles to commercial or ideological pressures. In the domain of the moral evaluation of war, apart from the militarist power-structures, whether of the Capitalist right or of the Communist left, the writers and the journalists have, on the whole, rendered significant service. Moral theologians owe them a debt.

But a still more important factor in the theological evaluation of war has been the massive increase in the destructiveness of modern weapons and in the frightfulness of modern war. The traditional theology of the just war was evolved in a different situation and was and is valid in that situation. It remains valid in principle still. But it becomes increasingly difficult to find application for it in the new situations of today.

It becomes more and more difficult today to find moral justification for war, any war. For both the philosophy and the practice of war today have become explicitly total; and the theology of the just war was precisely a formal repudiation of total war. The "total war" was always held by the Church to be as such unjust and evil. Pope John XXIII wrote, in *Pacem in Terris* :

> Men are becoming more and more convinced that disputes which arise between States should not be

resolved by recourse chiefly to arms but rather by negotiation . . . This conviction is based on the terrible destructive force of modern arms; and it is nourished by the horror aroused in the mind by the very thought of the cruel destruction and the immense suffering which the use of these armaments would bring to the human family. For this reason it is irrational to believe that in the atomic era war could any longer be regarded as a suitable means for restoring rights[1].

The Second Vatican Council similarly says than an entirely new evaluation of war is necessary in the changed conditions of today. It goes on :

This most holy Synod makes its own the condemnation of total war already pronounced by recent popes and issues the following declaration : Any act of war aimed indiscriminately at the destruction of entire cities or of extensive areas along with their populations is a crime against God and man himself. It merits unequivocal and unhesitating condemnation. The unique hazard of modern warfare consists in this : it provides those who possess modern scientific weapons with a kind of occasion for perpetrating just such abominations. Moreover, through a certain inexorable chain of events, it can urge on to the most atrocious decisions. *Gaudium et Spes,* 80.

EVIL CONSEQUENCES

An important element in any moral judgement is the evaluation of the consequences of an action. Our Lord himself said : "You will be able to tell them by their fruits." The fruits of war have been more and more clearly shown to be so poisonous that their evil almost inevitably outweighs any possible good that might be pursued through war.

From the purely expedient point of view, modern war has taken nearly all meaning out of the distinction between victors and vanquished. More seriously still, it can be said that very many of the moral and social evils of modern Europe and the modern world are the direct consequence of the disastrous world wars of this century or of the gross military budgets required by the balance of nuclear terror diplomacy practised by the great power blocs of East and West today.

WAR AND POLITICS

War, said Clausewitz, is diplomacy carried on by other means. The definition is famous but unfortunate. If a debate becomes heated and ends with fisticuffs or flick-knives, it would be paradoxical to say that the discussion was being carried on by other means. Rather, violence is the end of all rational discussion.

Similarly war is the failure of diplomacy. When war has done its worst, diplomacy must begin again; only now it is rendered even more difficult than before. War is the failure of politics; but when war is ended, politics has to take over the scorched earth. The so-called victors have to sacrifice their depleted resources to re-building the devastated cities and repairing the ruined economies of both sides. They have to devote their best energies for generations to reconciling the bitterness of the defeated and remedying the social and moral injuries sustained by themselves.

How much more rational and right it would be if the courage and virtue sacrificed in war were consecrated instead to politics. Politics is or should be the creator of civilisation and the builder of justice; war is the destroyer of civilisation and invariably a propagator of injustice. If civilisation be, as Whitehead defined it, the victory of persuasion over force, then war is the antithesis of civilisation.

THE DEMYTHOLOGISING OF REVOLUTIONARY VIOLENCE

All that we have said about war applies in due proportion to revolutionary violence. It is one of the sad paradoxes of our time that the "demythologising" of war has been accompanied by what amounts to a "remythologising" of revolutionary violence, whether of the social or nationalistic variety. The spurious glory and glamour which have been stripped from the brutal face of war have been often transferred to the no less brutal face of violent revolution. A new myth is being manufactured in our time — the myth of romantic revolution; and it corresponds exactly to the old and now discredited myth of romantic war.

As before, the ideologues and theoreticians are its promoters, the young and idealistic are its dupes, the weak and the little men, the children, the old and the defenceless are its victims.

Even some theologians are not immune from the spell of this myth. Even some priests can let themselves be exploited by ideologies of revolutionary violence, thus repeating all over again the same errors as some churchmen committed in past centuries when they let themselves be made the apologists of capitalist militarism.

A demythologising of revolutionary violence is urgently called for in our time. Writers, artists, journalists, as well as historians and sociologists have their part to play in this process. They, together with politicians on the one hand and theologians and pastors on the other, must collaborate in deepening our imaginative insight, improving our rational analysis, enlightening our conscience and raising the level of our political thought and action, so that we can morally repudiate violence, as we are learning to repudiate war, but without incurring the moral guilt of condoning the injustice that often motivates revolutionary violence, and without failing by a jot to match and indeed surpass the moral passion and the dedication to justice of the revolutionaries.

THE MORALITY OF VIOLENCE

The traditional teaching of the Church is clear and remains valid. It holds that in extreme situations of intolerable injustice, where no hope exists that peaceful and political action will secure the necessary reforms, violence may be the only means to secure justice. This teaching is, clearly, only a particular instance of the theology of the just war. But, like the theology of the just war, it needs to be re-examined in the changed conditions of today's world. This re-examination will show that both the methods and the consequences of revolutionary violence have so altered for the worse that, although sometimes justifiable in principle, violence can extremely rarely be justified in practice.

We are witnessing the emergence of a philosophy of total revolutionary violence, which corresponds exactly to the evil philosophy of total war and is equally intrinsically immoral. There is a spiralling rhythm of viciousness as between revolution and repression, which irresistibly impels towards the most brutal excesses and the most indiscriminate destruction. Once the momentum of violence is set in motion it becomes self-generating and is virtually impossible to stop.

In the case of revolutionary violence, it is the very fabric of civil society which is damaged, the very structures of social and economic development which are destroyed, perhaps even the very conditions of political consensus which are eliminated. The first victim of revolutionary violence, historically and logically, is likely to be democracy; and its first result is frequently military dictatorship.

IRISH REVOLUTIONARY EXPERIENCE

Truly terrible, therefore, is the responsibility of those who have recourse to revolutionary violence to achieve political or social ends. We in Ireland have often descanted on the "terrible beauty" born of our national struggle for independence. Perhaps we have so lyricised the beauty that we have forgotten the terror and the terrible cost.

I am personally convinced that our fight for national freedom was just and necessary. The heroism both of soldiers and civilians in that struggle wrote a glorious chapter in our history.

But honesty and realism forbid us to gloss over the heavy price the nation paid. Our total resources were exhausted for many years in repairing the physical destruction. It was decades before we were in a position to make any significant economic or social progress. It took a great part of the entire duration to date of our Independent State before the divisions left in the aftermath of the struggle could even begin to be healed and before divided former comrades could begin to speak to one another again. Our politics was for long polarised and dominated by the results of the struggle. We were for far too long so obsessed by recriminations about the revolutionary past that we were insensitive to the social problems of the present and dilatory in our planning for the future.

People who extol violence in the present situation in the North would do well to consider how closely set we could now be to a repetition of an almost identical pattern of division, polarisation, recrimination, social stagnation and economic regression over the next quarter or half-century.

POLITICS OR PHYSICAL FORCE?

A more balanced reading of our history would do greater justice to the contribution made to Irish freedom and Irish democracy by the non-physical-force movements. The whole constitutional, political and parliamentary tradition did as much as our soldier patriots to lay the foundations of the independent Irish State. Our legitimate pride in the Easter Proclamation must not make us less grateful to the Catholic Emancipation campaign, the Repeal Movement, the Land League and Tenant Right and Home Rule movements. We must not be less conscious of the importance of the Parnellite movement or less just to the Irish Parliamentary Party tradition.

A more enlightened approach to history will also bring us to see that Irish freedom was created by political skill and energy and dedication in the years that preceded it. As always, when the guns fall silent and the explosions cease, politics has to resume and rebuild.

The legitimate successors of the soldier patriots today are the men working for a more just Irish society. Irish freedom in many respects is still to be won. Servitude in the form of economic insecurity or social deprivation is still the lot of many Irishmen after fifty years of self-government.

DEMYTHOLOGISING IRISH HISTORY

The redressing of balance in the reading and teaching of Irish history has happily been energetically and effectively pursued in this country for at least thirty years now. Due recognition has rarely been given to the pioneer work done in this connection by the Department of History at University College, Dublin. Supported by the sister departments at our other university colleges, as well as by those of Trinity College, Dublin, and Queen's University, Belfast, these academic historians have made a powerful contribution to a salutary "demythologising" of national history.

The influence of the universities and of the secondary schools in this domain has not yet, however, reached all sectors of opinion or sufficiently pervaded politics and journalism

A STRATEGY OF NON-VIOLENCE

No one is better informed or more concerned than Pope Paul about the injustices existing and increasing in the modern world. Yet he firmly excludes violence as a solution, except perhaps in the most extreme cases:

> There are certainly situations whose injustice cries to heaven. When whole populations destitute of necessities live in a state of dependence barring them from all initiative and responsibility and all opportunity to advance culturally and share in social and political life, recourse to violence, as a means to right these wrongs to human dignity, is a grave temptation. We know, however, that a revolutionary uprising — save where there is manifest long-standing tyranny which would do great damage to fundamental personal rights and dangerous harm to the common good of the country — produces new injustices, throws more elements out of balance, and brings on new disasters. A real evil should not be fought against at the cost of greater misery. *Populorum Progressio,* 30.

One who lives closer to manifest and grievous injustice than most modern churchmen, namely the Brazilian Archbishop Dom Helder Camara, has never failed to couple his fearless denunciation of injustice and his insistent demand for reforms with advocacy of non-violence. We should hear in him one of the truly prophetic voices of our time when he says :

> My personal vocation is that of a pilgrim of peace, following the example of Paul VI; personally, I would prefer a thousand times to be killed than to kill. This personal position is based on the Gospel . . . It is enough to turn to the beatitudes — the quintessence of the Gospel message — to discover that the choice for Christians seems clear : we Christians are on the side of non-violence, which is by no means a choice of weakness or passivity. Non-violence means believing more passionately in the force of truth, justice and love than in the force of wars, murder and hatred[2].

Non-violence is not the coward's way. Its model is Christ, who died in the self-sacrificing act of a greater love than man has ever seen on earth. Its force is Christ, whose love was stronger than death, who is victoriously risen to live on and act on in our world for ever. Non-violence is not temporally and historically inactive or ineffectual. Its effectiveness, however, in man's struggle for justice and freedom has yet to be fully developed. Christians should take the lead in this development. Dom Helder Camara says elsewhere:

> Love alone constructs. Hatred and violence serve to destroy. . . . Personally I favour a large-scale experiment in non-racial integration led by Martin Luther King. . . . It is democratic and Christian to assist human weakness by a balanced, firm and just moral pressure based on non-violent action[3].

A Japanese layman, Dr Kinhide Mushakaji, addressing the recent Synod of Bishops, said:

> The incapacity of the existing structures to meet the demand of those who want more justice and more participation forces the latter into opting for violence. Although violent actions, street guerilla warfare, hijacking, etc., have a certain disturbing effect, they start a vicious circle of uprising and oppression in-

stead of achieving any constructive results. Indeed, the powerless betray their cause by using violence. They want to build a participatory society where there is no coercion and therefore no violence. To use violence is to deny this basic position and to fall into the trap prepared by their opponents. To promote a just and participatory society and to stop the proliferation of conflicts, it is therefore necessary to practice a non-violent action following in the footsteps of Mahatma Gandhi, Martin Luther King and Dom Helder Camara. . . . We must find a variable strategy of non-violent social change leading toward a more just and participatory society[4].

THE NORTHERN CRISIS

All that we have said finds ready application to the tragic situation in the North of Ireland. The bishops in the North have not failed in what is clearly their Christian duty — to condemn policies and acts of violence. But neither have they failed in their related Christian duty — to condemn the brutalities and inhumanities of military repression, which provokes further injustices, and to call for political reforms to remove the basic injustices out of which the violence grew. They have not been cultivating a public image, but trying to perform a duty in conscience before God — and have therefore not sought to publicise the constant and insistent representations they have been making to the responsible authorities to impress on them the need to abandon ruinous policies and be seen to be implementing radical structural reforms.

Denunciation of violence has been, is and will continue to be utterly ineffectual, so long as the policies which provoke violence are persisted in. The sooner this is realised by the responsible authorities, above all in Westminster, where the true initiative and the real responsibility lie, the better for both our countries. It

is futile and self-contradictory for the authorities to
expect violence to cease when the only methods they
seem capable of using to combat violence are themselves
infected by all the poison of the very same violence. If
there ever was any doubt, it should now be plain to all
that internment, with its accompanying and inherent
inhumanities, raids, house searches and harassment of
entire Catholic communities, are daily advancing the
cause of violence. Surely British politicians are capable
of wiser counsels that those they have followed in
Ireland in the last year.

It is no use holding out promises of structural reforms
when the violence ends; there is no hope whatever of
the violence ending unless the reforms are worked out
and put into effect first. It is no use talking vaguely of
a "permanent, active and guaranteed role" for the
minority unless this talk is translated into visable and
operative structures now. The crisis in the North is
basically a crisis of credibility and confidence. These
will not be restored by speeches or promises, much less
by threats, but only by political acts.

The welfare of both our countries is at stake. All the
hopes of understanding and collaboration between this
country and Britian, slowly and laboriously built up in
recent years, are put gravely in danger by the present
situation in the North. Unless non-violence is given a
chance, by the political leaders who alone have the
power to give it a chance, the future in this island and
indeed even in the neighbouring one, is grim indeed.
But non-violence can conquer violence only through
reforms. Immediately after excluding violence as a
solution, Pope Paul continues:

> We want to be clearly understood: the present situa-
> tion must be faced with courage and the injustices
> linked with it must be fought against and overcome.

Development demands bold transformations, innovations that go deep. Urgent reforms must be undertaken without delay. It is for each one to take his share in them with generosity, particularly those whose education, position and opportunities afford them wide scope for action. *Populorum Progressio,* 32.

RESPONSIBILITY OF IRISH POLITICANS
Irish politicians, both North and South, have also a grave responsibility in the present crisis. No more serious problem has confronted them since the foundation of this State. Politicans here need to acquire a close, accurate knowledge of the realities of the Northern situation, an intimate understanding of the Northern traditions and the Northern mind, both Protestant and Catholic. This they cannot acquire without continuous contact with Northern representatives. They must have detailed and thoroughly-researched and realistic plans for both short-term reforms and long-term solutions. Minority leaders in the North must try, despite the superhuman difficulties, to reach agreed, viable and effective proposals for the talks which must some time replace the guns and the bombs, the rubber bullets, C.S. gas and internment camps. Theirs will be the work of true patriots. Irish political leaders, acting wisely as servants of Christian justice and love in this crisis, can earn a place in history as noble as that of the founders of this State. Their responsibility is hardly less great.

PRAYER FOR PEACE
But simultaneously with all this, we are continuously conscious that "unless the Lord watches over the city, they labour in vain who keep watch". Pope John — the first Pope whose passing was mourned as a personal sorrow in the Protestant streets of Belfast — said:

(The work of peace) is such a noble and elevated

task that human resources . . . cannot bring it to realisation alone . . . Help from on high is necessary. (May Christ, the prince of peace) banish from the hearts of men whatever might endanger peace, may he transform them into witnesses of truth, justice and brotherly love. May he enlighten the rulers of peoples so that, in addition to their solicitude for the proper welfare of their citizens, they may guarantee and defend the great gift of peace; may he enkindle the wills of all, so that they may overcome the barriers that divide, cherish the bonds of mutual charity, understand others, and pardon those who have done them wrong; by virtue of his action, may all peoples of the earth become as brothers, and may the most longed-for peace blossom forth and reign always between them. *Pacem in Terris,* p. 62.

Our prayer will have a special fervour and efficacity when it is directed to God through the intercession of Mary, Queen of Peace. It is striking to read these days the words of the prophet Isaiah, which we read in our Advent liturgy:

The merry tambourines are silent,
the sound of revelling is over,
the merry lyre is silent.
They no longer sing over their wine . . .
The city of emptiness is in ruins,
the entrance to every house is shut.
There is lamentation in the streets: no wine,
joy quite gone,
gladness banished from the country.
Nothing but rubble in the city,
the gate smashed to pieces (*Isaiah* 24 : 8-12).

Isaiah is referring to the desolation of the earth before the coming of the Prince of Peace. But these verses of Isaiah are deliberately recalled and reversed in the gospel of St John, in the description of the miracle at Cana in Galilee. At the prayer of Mary, Christ changes everything. The water becomes wine, exuberant, abundant, unsurpassed. Lamentation is changed into joy and gladness spreads through the land.

By the power of Christ and the prayer of his mother, so may it be again in our day, in the rubble-strewn cities and the strife-torn communities of the North. The standard of patriotism for the Christian must always be, not how much have I fought, but how many have I helped?; not how bravely have I served in battle, but how powerfully have I served love? In the evening of life, we shall all be judged on love.

The Spiral of Violence

From an Address at the Annual Dinner of the Longford Association in London, November 10th, 1971.

It is no alarmism but simple realism to recognise that Ireland as a whole is passing at the present time through the most serious crisis since our Civil War. If the present vicious spiral of violence and repression continues, the entire island could be plunged into anarchy and chaos.

The whole achievement of half a century of freedom, our hardwon democratic structures, our incipient and fragile economic progress, all are threatened by every bomb exploding in the North, as well as by every maltreated internee and shot civilian. Irish emotions are rising to near danger level at the present time. But our democratic institutions cost our fathers too much for us to let them be flaunted by people who exploit our emotions in order to deaden our reason.

FALSE ANALOGY WITH 1916

For, even apart from Christian principle, our reason must tell us that the present brutal confrontation of violences in the North can only lead in the end to the emergence of two Irish civilian militia forces confronting one another across barricades of permanent hate and a no-man's-land of rubble. An escalation of emotional approval of violence in the Republic could bring real danger of an armed putsch, of which the first casualty would be Irish democracy. We know only too well from recent world history the sort of power that can grow out of the barrels of guns.

It will be retorted that modern Irish democracy grew precisely out of the barrels of the rifles of 1916. But let us never forget that that revolutionary violence was endorsed and the subsequent struggle legitimated by the most democratic and most conclusive election perhaps ever held in Ireland. The army that fought for freedom was the Army of the elected Parliament and government of the Irish people. It fought precisely to establish the patriotic and democratic principle that only an Irish Parliament had the right to establish an Irish Army or to commit the Irish people to a war. That is one of the most sacrosanct principles of the Irish republican tradition. To violate it is to betray the whole tradition.

The setting up of that Parliament and Government was not seen as the end of Ireland's struggle but as its beginning. It was the precondition for the more important permanent revolution of creating an Ireland in which every citizen would have a right "to an adequate share of the produce of the nation's labour"; an Ireland in which "no child shall suffer hunger or cold from lack of food or clothing or shelter"; an Ireland which shall devise "a sympathetic native scheme for the care of the nation's aged and infirm"; an Ireland committed to a programme of "social and industrial legislation (to effect) . . . general and lasting improvements in the conditions under which the working classes live and labour"; the Ireland, in other words, of the Democratic Programme of the first Dáil. It is this Ireland, with its limited but real achievements and its noble hopes, which is being put at risk by the present violence and its emotional repercussions.

MORALITY OF VIOLENCE

A Christian is not obliged to hold that recourse to violence is in all circumstances and of necessity wrong. In extreme situations of intolerable injustice, where no hope exists that peaceful and political action will secure reforms, violence may be the only means to secure justice. But grave indeed are the consequences of recourse to violence and heavy is the responsibility of those who resort to it. It took us most of fifty years to recover from the divisions, suspicions and bitternesses left behind in the wake of our just struggle for national independence; and some of the effects still remain as a constant threat to Irish democracy.

The immediate effects of the present violence in the North represent already a crushing burden of human tragedy. One has only to think of the wrecked and ravaged little homes, the nerve-racked mothers, the hysterical children, the terrified old and ill, the worried wives and families of internees.

Speaking in London as an Irish bishop and priest, I welcome the opportunity of expressing heartfelt sympathy with the wives and families of the young British soldiers who have lost their lives in what must have seemed to them a senseless and incomprehensible conflict. I express the same deep sympathy with the bereaved wives and families of Ulster policemen.

Unless peace is restored, and quickly, nothing but anarchy, unemployment, poverty and disintegration of society can result. Violence will become a way of life for many and can permanently warp the personalities of youth. The effects could be with us for decades, in terms of violent crime, gangsterism, lawlessness and psycho-social illness.

Nothing can justify the present campaign of violence;

it is morally evil and opposed to every Christian principle. If the end is asserted to be the reunification of Ireland, violence is immediately seen to be irrational as well as evil. When the real national problem is one of establishing mutual peace and trust between different communities within Ireland, talk of violent solutions is self-contradictory. Force as a solution to the present Irish problem must be unconditionally condemned and renounced.

SPIRAL OF VIOLENCE AND REPRESSION

But the violence of repression must be equally pronounced irrational and evil. The whole lesson of recent post-colonial history is that urban political violence cannot be stamped out by counter-violence.

Dom Helder Camara, Archbishop of Recife, Brazil, has spoken on the "spiral of violence". He shows how "violence No. 1", the "established violence" of injustice, provokes "violence No. 2", the violence of revolt, and this in turn leads to "violence No. 3", repression, internment, torture. So the spiral goes on, and it is an escalating one, with repression provoking reprisals and these calling forth more violent repression and so on. Dom Helder concludes that "the only true answer to violence is to have the courage to face the injustices which constitute violence No. 1".

POLITICAL REFORMS

This is the courage which is called for from all those responsible for the Northern Ireland situation today. Repressive measures are obviously ineffectual. Moral denunciations of violence and appeals for reconcilation, though they are our Christian duty and must be unwearyingly persevered with, are inefficacious. Political measures of a radical nature are our only hope.

Ways must be found of assuring the minority of a share, as of right, in political responsibility and decision-making power. A minority is insulted in its human dignity when it is permanently excluded from participation in the government of its own society or when its members can hope for access to that participation only on condition of changing their political affiliation. No economic or social benefit will ever assuage the insult of the denial of political equality. This is the first truth that must be grasped by all those concerned with the Irish Question today.

Courageous and lasting initiatives must be taken by political leaders to create the conditions, the institutions and the structures in which the minority can feel their political equality and their civil rights guaranteed. And they must be taken soon. We could borrow the words of Pope Paul from *Populorum Progressio* and say: "Development demands bold transformation, innovations that go deep. Urgent reforms should be undertaken without delay." Political and social leaders must face up to these issues as one of the gravest problems which have confronted statesmen in both parts of Ireland and in Britain in recent history. May these leaders prove worthy of the challenge and the urgency of this hour.

RECIPROCAL TRUST
In a sense it is the whole truth and the only truth to say that we must love one another. But the Christian command to love includes the political command to remove the conditions which make love difficult and to create the structures which enable love and trust and mutual tolerance to grow.

Catholics must make a determined and sustained effort to understand the minds and the emotions, be they fears or suspicions or prejudices, of Protestants; and Protestants those of Catholics reciprocally. The tragedy of our present situation is that the incipient growth of understanding and mutual acceptance which marked the ten years up to August 1969, has now been blighted by the frost of violence. The contribution which each of our traditions has made and can make to the good of our land is being stunted by present hatreds, to the loss of Ireland and the detriment of Britain as well.

Since I came to live in the Republic, I have experienced a total absence of political sectarianism, a warm and spontaneous social ecumenism, which provide a sense of liberation from the old inhibitions and give to life a new dimension of kindly graciousness. What an enrichment all Ireland will receive when this spirit can be spread throughout the whole land.

THE IRISH PROTESTANT TRADITION

As one who lived all my life up to four years ago in the North of Ireland, I can speak from experience and without reserve of the value for Ireland of the Church of Ireland and Presbyterian tradition. I have worked for a quarter of a century with Northern Protestant colleagues in Queen's University, Belfast, and have never worked with men of greater integrity. If one seeks proof of what Ulster Protestants can offer, one need look no further than that University, which I claim to be one of the best and most enlightened and most liberal universities in these islands. The people who created Queen's, the people whose forebears contributed so powerfully to the democratic freedoms of the United States of America, have certainly intelligence enough, integrity and sense of justice enough to create genuinely democratic and tolerant and participatory institutions at home.

One of my heroes as a university student was that great Northern Protestant Irishman, Professor Robert Michael Henry. He in turn fired me with youthful admiration for that outstanding Christian minister who was the Presbyterian Reverend J. B. Armour of Ballymoney. I shall end with the hope of Armour of Ballymoney:

> I am sure that a race of Presbyterians and Protestants worthy of the best traditions of our faith will arise in the future . . . (who will) . . . claim to dwell in the land, not under the protection of the Saxon, not by permission of the Celt, but in virtue of the services they will render to a country which we love and for whose welfare we pray.

The tragedy of the present violence is that it so damages and defers the fulfilment of that splendid hope as to make the heart sick.

Christian Patriotism in Ireland now

Address to the Armagh Catholic Teachers' Guild, meeting in Dundalk on May 20th, 1972.

One of the most serious challenges to Christian patriotism in Ireland for many decades is the continuing disorder in the North. Two months after the Heath initiative, we seem as far as ever from even the beginning of preliminaries to talks. Yet talks must one day replace the green and the orange varieties of mindless militarism, and the bombings and the shootings which are now being done more from habit or ignorance of any alternative, than from policy.

Even those who tried to justify the violence of recent years in military terms surely have to admit that military violence is never an end in itself. It is at best a means to political settlement. Even if Clausewitz's dictum were true, that war is diplomacy carried on by other means, the converse would be equally true, that the purpose of war must be to restore the normal operations of diplomacy when the proper conditions of diplomacy have been re-established. Surely, since the Westminster initiative, these conditions now exist.

OUTDATED SLOGANS

Why then is it that the hoped-for atmosphere for talks and negotiation is as far away as ever? It is in large part because the reason and the conscience of so many on both sides are paralysed by outdated slogans. The thinking of many activists in both republican and unionist extremist camps is frozen at a pre-rational stage in the deep freeze of fifty years ago.

Almost every thing in Europe has changed in the last half century. Queen Elizabeth is visiting France, which used to call England "perfidious Albion" and which, only a few years ago, blocked England's entry into the EEC. Germany and Britain, implacable enemies of two World Wars, are now preparing to be partners in a Community of Europe in which war will be unthinkable. For this is 1972, not 1912 and not 1922. One is tempted to say that in Europe almost everything has changed in fifty years — except Ulster unionism and militant Irish republicanism. If they do not both change quickly, even Europe will not be able to save Ireland from its own death-wish.

Republicans might surely learn from the present plight of unionism the folly of clinging to outdated slogans. Unionism tried to enter the 1970s with the policies and attitudes of the 1910s. Hence its present discomfiture and disarray. Unless republicanism moves away from its obsession with an anachronistic militarism and physical force, the Ireland they speak of liberating could become a grave of liberty and a grave of democracy.

"GET THE BRITISH OUT"
We need to have the honesty and the courage to have a fresh look at each of these fifty-year-old slogans. "Get the British out" needs to be re-examined, as much as "Ulster is British." "Never trust the British" needs a new scrutiny as much as does "No surrender". Indeed, these slogans, apparently opposite to one another, really betray a fundamentally identical mentality.

The slogan "Ulster is British" commits the basic error that has flawed all unionism throughout its history — it simply ignores the existence of half a million people living *in* that Ulster who are not *of* that kind of Ulster. Stormont failed because it ignored the existence of the Ulster which is Irish and is determined to remain Irish.

But the republican slogan "Get the British out" commits an exactly similar error — that of ignoring the existence of nearly a million Ulstermen who see themselves as not only Irishmen but also in a sense very real to them as British. The final logic of "getting the British out" might be found to entail "getting out" those Irish who have British loyalties — or at least getting them "out" of those loyalties by bombs and bullets. But surely the very history of Irish nationalism shows that loyalties cannot be crushed by bombs or bullets?

MYTH OF THE "FIGHTING IRISH"

Ulster unionists cannot be coerced. They can be persuaded. The task will be demanding, slow, difficult. It would be to take a poor view of the Irish to think they were not capable of the task.

It was always the old-style British colonialist or imperialist who liked to say the Irish were good at killing — and so they invented the myth of the "fighting Irish" and sent Irish regiments around all frontiers of the empire to do their killing. The Irish, they said, were good at killing, but no good at thinking, reasoning, convincing. Have republicans now come to think the same thing? Does one prove one's Irishness and one's patriotism by the accuracy of one's fire-power and the destructiveness of one's bombs? Is the good Irishman the Irishman who is good at killing?

Another of the slogans of fifty years ago which is still

invoked is "Never trust the British." It belongs to the same category as "Never trust the Fenians", or even "There are no good Germans only dead Germans." Such slogans spell nothing but ruin for their authors. A slogan which was popular in Britain and America during the war years was "Unconditional Surrender." It seemed emotionally satisfying but it cost the Allies dear. It prolonged the war by months, perhaps years, and cost countless Allied as well as German lives. Hate is the surest way to self-mutilation.

SOLUTIONS NOT SLOGANS

We have thought our slogans were solutions, instead of which they were only statements of our problems. The slogan : "Withdrawal of British support from Ulster" is thought to be a solution. Instead it merely underlines the difficulty and points to a problem. The difficulty is that the industry and the agriculture, the jobs and the incomes, the factories and the market outlets, the standards of education, health services and welfare of the people, both Protestant and Catholic, both unionist and nationalist, in the North of Ireland at present depend massively on British financing. The problem is: how can these be assured after British withdrawal?

The problem is not insoluble but it is no help to ignore it. Patriotic oratory will not talk it away. Bullets and bombs will not blast it away. Instead one wonders if the republican militants somehow assume that the British will still be around to rebuild the factories, take care of the unemployment, and repair the destruction caused by their bombs. It is hard to see how we would be able to do it ourselves.

The slogan: "Create an Irish Socialist Workers' Republic" is presented as a solution. Instead, it too underlines a difficulty and states a problem. The difficulty is that nearly a million Irishmen in the North, the majority of them workers, want nothing of such a Republic. The problem, for those who use this slogan, is how to persuade them to accept it. Chanting the slogan at mass meetings of non-unionists will not change the situation.

Once the unionist workers have been persuaded, next the nationalist workers and then the voters in the Republic will have to be persuaded, since it must be presumed that they are not going to be coerced. I mention this, because it seems to me an example of how the new "scientific socialist" thinking about Irish problems can resemble the old sentimentalist rhetoric of many Irish political platforms. We seem to have a persistent propensity in Ireland to blur the hard edges of real problems by the smoke screens of our own fine talk.

PATRIOTISM AND PSEUDO-PATRIOTISM

It is the work of true patriotism to think through and beyond the slogans to the hard grit of the problems of Irish unity. Such thinking must surely show that violence is now an irrelevance and indeed an obstacle to a solution of the problem.

There has been a serious fallacy in much recent discussion about violence in Ireland now. The argument has often been about the justification or otherwise of violence in principle as a protest against injustice. But in the North of Ireland we are not talking about violence in principle, or violence in the abstract. We are talking about tactics and strategies of violence, used by physical-force republicans for certain stated and specific aims, which are summed up in the reunification of Ireland. It is in this context and as a means to these ends that violence has to be justified.

Those who use it have a duty to show how violence can

be related to these ends and specifically how violence can secure that a million unionists will consent to live peacefully in a United Ireland. Against whom precisely is the violence being directed and for what precise purpose? In the context of reuniting Ireland, violence could be designed only either to coerce the unionists into submission, or to force the British into coercing the unionists into submission. Each of these two aims is impossible; and, even if either were possible, it would be immoral. I do not hesitate, therefore, to say that the use of physical force as a means of reuniting Ireland is immoral.

DANGER OF SECTARIAN CIVIL WAR

Indeed the frightening evidence is accumulating daily that the most likely result of physical force, if it continues, is a sectarian civil war which can bring disaster to this country as great as our worst invaders ever brought to it. One cannot help wondering, indeed, whether some may be perverted to the point of planning to bring this about. Republicans protest that they are non-sectarian and want a non-sectarian Ireland. Deeds speak louder than words.

Words will not unite when the deeds of those who speak them drive divisions deeper. It is no use saying that sectarian conflict is not one's intention when sectarian conflict is the almost inevitable result of one's acts. One is morally responsible before God not only for what one intends but for the certain or probable consequences of what one does. If a civil war situation were to develop, those who organised the violence, and particularly those who decided that it must continue after the Westminster initiative, will bear a heavy share in the responsibility for what could be an unparalleled national catastrophe.

APPEAL TO REPUBLICANS

I am not saying that they would have the sole responsibility. But to have even part responsibility for such a shocking prospect is something that I certainly would not like to have on my conscience. I cannot believe that republicans who stop seriously to think, alone with their conscience, alone before God, can go on incurring this fearsome responsibility.

I can sympathise with the feelings of militants in the republican tradition. Like most nationally-minded Irish youth, I once shared their emotions. Indeed, I regret to say, I once in my youth shared their passions, some of their inherited hates. I still share many of the ideals of their tradition. It is because their commitment to physical force is so destructive of those ideals, that I believe present republican policies are a betrayal of the true republican tradition and are, as of now, a menace to the Irish nation. The dead generations of Irish patriots would abjure them. Future generations of Irishmen will not forgive them if they persist in their disaster course.

To say that methods are disastrous is not necessarily to say that those who use them are wicked. Even to say that methods are immoral is not necessarily to say that those who use them are evil. Many of these men are sincere idealists who see themselves as in the line of Ireland's patriot dead. Many have proved their sincerity by high courage. Many have risked liberty, limb and life in the service of their cause. Many have made the supreme sacrifice of their lives for their ideals. The indiscriminate use of the term "terrorist" for men who see themselves as patriots has been deeply resented.

THE IDEALS OF 1916

It is in the name of their patriotism that I would appeal

to them to stop and think before their actions bring the country over the brink of disaster. True patriotism now is non-violent. In a sense, as Pope Paul said of peace, its true name now is development — social, economic, community and inter-community development. The man of true courage in Ireland now is the man who speaks peace across the misnamed "peace-line", which instead is the badge of our shameful hates.

When someone condemns violence in Ireland now it is often charged that he must consequently condemn the violence used by the patriots of 1916. The charge is unfounded. I am not condemning the rising of 1916. I am simply saying that this is not 1916. This is 1972. The patriotism of 1916 must change, if it is to be true patriotism for 1972.

Patriotism is an unchanging commitment to the service of a nation. But it is not abstract devotion to an ideal nation, but real service of real people in their real needs now. The methods which were patriotic in 1916 or 1921 can be anti-patriotic now. The true continuance of the Irish republican tradition of 1916-1921 will consist now in peaceful, constructive, political commitment to the creation of the new Ireland of the democratic Programme of the First Dáil. This will be an Ireland which unionists cannot indeed be coerced into accepting, but can gradually be persuaded to accept, or rather to help us to build. As has been very well said by someone in a different context, we cannot go back on the principles of the men of 1916, but we can go forward from them.

INTERNMENT

To go forward in Ireland, forward from 1912 and from 1916, forward from 1969, and forward from the Westminster initiative, will call for cool and resolute courage from all concerned. Those now responsible for government and security in the North will be under heavy and understandable pressure to slow down the release of internees, to resume military repression. These measures must be firmly resisted. Either of these steps would be disastrous. Military counter-violence and internment have been the greatest promoters of physical-force republicanism. They are still its strongest argument and the source of its greatest appeal. Not only the brutal treatment of many internees but the very fact of internment itself has extended bitterness into areas previously peaceful, and spread alienation across the entire nationally-minded population.

Indeed internment is having another and paradoxical effect. Internment has often removed from communities the more respected, more responsible and more moderate representatives of nationalist opinion. It has thus left leadership in the hands of younger, more immature and more reckless and sometimes irresponsible elements. I am convinced that the speedy and unconditional release of all internees and detainees would at the present time be a force for non-violence instead of for violence. It might well be the catalyst which could transform our situation from one of near despair into one of refound hope. I am of course including Protestant "political prisoners" in this category too.

The release of internees must, and I am confident would, be accompanied by a resolute effort by all community leaders in the alienated areas to ensure massive popular repudiation of acts of violence and of men and methods of physical force — provided, of course, that the persistent and real fear in these areas of attacks from armed so-called "loyalists" were removed.

BRITISH WITHDRAWAL
The cry to the British to "get out" is perhaps somewhat

ironical at the present time. It is quite probable that the British would like nothing better than to "get out" of Ireland now. Involvement with the Irish problem now is burdensome and probably distasteful for their Army, injurious to their overseas prestige and damaging to their international influence. Policies of military repression and security interrogation have lessened their credibility, strained their moral sense, twisted their moral vocabulary. They would and will gladly "get out" of Ireland. But they will get out, not when we Irish force them, but when we Irish let them; that is to say, when they can leave without abandoning us to the dangers of self-destruction.

TIME OF OPPORTUNITY

The dramatic events of March 23rd ushered in a new opportunity. The British initiative, for which we all called so insistently, has come; and in all honesty we have to admit that it has been more courageous and more far-reaching than any of us ever anticipated. All that any true Emmet or Tone or Davis patriot ever dreamt of as a long-term hope for a pluriform but ultimately united Ireland is now possible. But it is possible only on condition that all concerned rise to the level of the occasion.

It is surely anomalous that a country which has had for fifty years for its final national aim the "reintegration of the national territory" has no Minister or Department for Northern Affairs, and is only now, nearly three years after August 1969, setting up an inter-party Committee on the North. But there is no time for recriminations or regrets. The danger is now.

Now that the EEC issue is settled, the country must unitedly concentrate on its major national problem, the crisis in the North. Party politics can take second place in this time of national crisis. The lesson of our EEC negotiations is relevant and is encouraging. It was a notable success for Irish negotiating skill. It took ten years and more to accomplish.

But there is no reason to doubt that if we devote the same skill, pertinacity, intelligence and conviction, together with the same not only two-party but all-party cooperation, over the next ten years, to building adequate and just social structures and working out conditions for offering Ulster unionists partnership in a new Ireland, we can bring that aim into the range of feasibility and within sight of fulfilment. History never offered a nobler challenge, and, in spite of all our present woes and fears, never presented a finer opportunity to Irishmen.

Christian Leadership in Ireland now

Address at the opening of a Seminar on Religious Life in Our Lady's Bower Convent, Athlone, on July 10th, 1972.

With the break-down of the uneasy truce of the past fortnight, we meet in the shadow and in the fear of what the coming days and weeks may bring.

Leaders have not even yet appreciated the enormity of their responsibility. In the North, those who ought to have been giving mature and responsible leadership to a confused and apprehensive majority population have instead played upon their fears, heightened their insecurity, inflamed fear into fanaticism. They could, while it was still only the eleventh hour, have begun preparing their followers for the building of a new society. Instead, they led the way backwards to the wastelands of old prejudices and primitive and regressive emotions. They have misused language to darken counsel, calling lawlessness loyalty and anarchy law, confused naked sectarianism with patriotism.

May Christian leaders at least have the vision and the courage at this twenty-fourth hour to try to pull people who call themselves Christians back from the brink of mutual destruction. May they begin now, while there is yet time, if there is still time, to give Christian witness, at the cost of whatever unpopularity, insult or opposition it may bring, to the full demands of Christian truth and love and to the full dimensions of Christian peace and order in our present situation. The unqualified and bilateral renunciation of violence as a means to political ends, accompanied by the vigorous re-education of all Christian groups in Ireland in their evaluation of physical force as a political weapon is an urgent duty laid upon the consciences of all Christian leaders at the present time.

The Christian call to love applies not only in the realm of neighbour-to-neighbour reconciliation and friendship. Love which is Christian demands that society be restructured so that the obstacles to Christian reconciliation and love be removed, and the political, social and economic conditions of love and brotherhood be created. The barricades in the North were political and social and economic before they became physical. The physical barricades simply reflect society as it has been shaped by its leaders and allowed to be shaped by its beneficiaries for fifty years. You cannot remove political and social and economic barricades by talk of Christian love, without Christian political and social action.

The task of Christian leadership now is to educate people, fearlessly and energetically, into acceptance of the radical changes of thinking, of attitude and of political structures that are necessary if peace is to come to the Northern communities and to our whole island. It would have been foolish to think that we had peace in the past fortnight. But what the people demanded and were entitled to receive was peace to work for peace, peace to begin to dig foundations for the building of a peaceful, because just, society. Nobody had any right to welcome a backward-looking peace. Nobody was or is justified in expecting a restoration of the past.

What we desperately need now is peace again to work for peace. May Christians in all churches take the lead in creating readiness for this work of building peace. May they do it with the urgency and the boldness of the love of Christ which should impel and compel us. Our love as Christians is not a matter of words and emotions. The love we believe in was crucified. We cannot expect witness to love on other conditions or to be peace-makers on any easier terms.

May the example of Fr Hugh Mullen and Fr Noel Fitzpatrick, two priests who have died for the sake of their ministry of reconciliation, help us all, and their example inspire us all, to eradicate from our whole society the seeds of hate which are now producing these bitter grapes of wrath, and plant instead, in deep furrows in the minds and consciences of all for whom we have a responsibility in Christ, the seeds of Christian love and brotherhood, dignity, equality and justice.

May unionists have the courage and true patriotism to renounce the evil ways of hooded men and to detach themselves from leaders who can only lead the province they love to undying disgrace and ruin.

May republicans hear the pleas of the people of the narrow streets and the crippled ghettos and renounce violence. They have a choice now, and a responsibility to all Ireland and before future Irish history for the choice they make. They can choose between a Union of Ireland in the future with consent and consensus, if they have the patience to wait for it and the dedication and the conviction to work for it and to deserve it, and an island of misery and anarchy now, with hopes of unity deferred for another weary half-century.

Christian Peace:
The Challenge to the Individual

A lecture to the 20th Summer School of the Social Study Conference, Falcarragh, Co. Donegal, on August 11th, 1972.

MYSTICAL REPUBLICANISM

Physical-force Republicans and their sympathisers, to refer to them first, have for the most part invoked the principles of the just revolution in order to justify their use of violence. Violence, they argue, is the only means available to them to overthrow an unjust and undemocratic regime and to secure justice and democracy for an oppressed minority.

Admittedly this sort of reasoning is not the sole or even the main component in republican psychology. Underlying it and much more potent than it is the romantic-mystical love of the Republic, nobly rescued from captivity by her soldier sons, and the tragical-mystical memories of the Republic betrayed again by the politicians. Out of this emotional substratum grows the conviction of a nation's task unfinished, a national duty reneged, and of this generation's call to complete the mission the politicians have betrayed, by driving the usurper from the last of Ireland's four green fields.

Before the emotional-mystical source of this republican psychology, one must have deep respect. Our past struggle for freedom was inspired and sustained by it.

And that struggle was no babble of fools. It embodied much of what is best in our history.

It is rather otiose to speculate now as to whether Irish freedom might have been obtained without violence. The fact that in the circumstances it was not obtained without violence is perhaps the only sort of proof history recognises that it could not have been obtained without violence. History is to do with what did in fact happen, not with what might have happened. If great powers would learn from history, history would be very different. But one thing we do indisputably learn from history is that the great and powerful never learn from history.

Alas, neither do the weak and the small. One thing we Irish have still to learn from our own history is the terrible cost of violence, even of justifiable violence in a good and noble cause. Nearly all of the gravest problems which have beset us in this country for the past fifty years derive from the fact that we were obliged to resort to violence in order to secure our just freedom — even though we were morally right to resort to violence for that just cause.

Only one of the prices paid for nationalistic violence is the mythical glorification and glamorisation of violence. Patriotic violence cannot succeed without creating the mystique of romantic nationalism or romantic revolution. But once created, this mystique becomes a mythology which distorts history, undermines constructive patriotism and endangers democracy. Shooting comes to appear more pure, honourable and noble than politics; the only true patriotism is thought to be that of the soldier or freedom-fighter. There is always an appeal beyond actual loyalty to the actual Republic to allegiance to the Ideal Republic; from the living Republic to the Republic of the dead patriots; an appeal beyond the wishes and the welfare of the real living people in the real Ireland to the Mystical Ireland of the dead generations — in short, beyond democracy to the gun.

Such a mystique is utterly impervious to reasoning or to rebuttal by empirical fact — even the massive and democratically decisive fact of disavowal by the Irish electorate. Hence two political organisations and two private armies can claim exclusive legitimate succession from the Irish Republic of 1916-1921, but so far as the Irish Republic of 1972 is concerned, have little else in common with one another except their contempt for and their intent to overthrow its freely and democratically elected government and parliament — not to mention their contempt for, and policy to thwart and supplant the democratically elected representatives of the nationally-minded Northern minority.

The persistence of this mystique of the patriotic rifle has been and remains one of the most serious threats to Irish democracy. It is a legacy of the sad necessity of recourse to arms in defence of justice and freedom. It would, in any case, have been difficult to eradicate. But it might well have been largely absorbed by now, were it not for the unjust and unworkable solution imposed by Britain upon Ireland in 1921.

One claim at least of the republicans is true, that political violence will never be removed from Irish society, North or South, until a just and acceptable solution is found for the problem of the North, a solution endorsed by bilateral consent and productive of community consensus, to replace a solution which, after fifty years of trial, has proved itself a failure.

NORTHERN VIOLENCE NOW

Violence in the North today is, of course, bi-partisan.
I shall speak of unionist violence in a moment. Republican violence is seen by its authors and defenders
as a continuation of the struggle for national freedom,
a completion of the unfinished business of the national
revolution of fifty years ago. This is the point of depar-
ture of the argument that republican violence is justified because it fulfils the conditions for a just revolution.

Where this argument fails is in its refusal to see that
the national problem today is radically different from
that of fifty years ago and the methods which were
necessary and right then are simply not relevant now.
The obstacle now to freedom, for that part of the
population of the "fourth green field" which is unfree,
is not British imperialist occupation of a part of Ireland,
but the presence there of nearly a million Irishmen who
do not feel unfree because they do not share our concept
of freedom or of nationhood.

Yet, if we really believe in a united Ireland they too
are our people, Irish people, not foreign invaders or
alien occupiers of our land. They are not colonists who
could be repatriated. This was and is their homeland;
they know and seek no other. This land is their land,
by virtue of more than three centuries of loving hus-
bandry and industrial skill and civic virtue. Any solution to the problem of the North must begin by recognising their right to exist and their right to share
Ireland with us, without having to give up their own
political, cultural and national traditions; including
their right to refuse to share the republican view of
Irish history or the republican concept of Irish nationhood. The analogies with 1916 are misleading today.
The methods of 1916 are counter-productive today.

Republican violence, in recent years and months, has, with total predictability, made the rift between the two communities in the North more unbridgeable than ever it has been in the life-time of any inhabitant of the Six Counties. It has made the task of bringing about peaceful coexistence between unionists and nationalists, not to speak of the bringing about of unity between them in one nation, more agonisingly difficult than ever it has been.

Completion of Ireland's struggle now can only be the patient effort of persuasion, the persevering labour of politics, the intelligent practice of diplomacy. Violence now is the expression of frustration and fanaticism, where what is needed is hope and intelligence, mutual trust and mutual respect, tolerance, confidence in reason and in dialogue.

FROM FORCE TO PERSUASION

Whitehead defined civilisation as the substitution of persuasion for force. The cynical view which tends to be bred by a national myth of violence is that force is the only argument that imperialists will ever understand. This view has to be seriously questioned in the actual circumstances of Ireland and Britain in the 1970s.

Even in the different circumstances of fifty years ago, when imperialism was incomparably more morally unchallenged and more ruthless than it is today, force alone would never have freed Ireland, but for the pressure of world opinion and but for the conscience of liberal friends of Ireland in Britain, for Irish republicans then were able to persuade both of the justice of their cause. The only hope of effecting a just solution of the Irish problem now lies in persuading world opinion and the conscience of the British public that the nationalist case against unionism is just.

PUBLIC OPINION

Three years ago and until perhaps one year ago, world opinion and British opinion were convinced of the injustice of the Stormont regime and more concerned to see justice done than they had been even of Ireland's right to freedom fifty years ago. But, in the more recent past, world opinion has been sickened and sympathies in Britain alienated — and this precisely by the intransigence and the ruthlessness of republican violence. Force which cannot persuade and seems not even to try can only be brutal and brutalise its authors. Force which outrages moral conscience can never set people free.

Some words of Senator Edward Kennedy, in his March, 1970 address on Burke to the College Historical Society in Trinity College, Dublin, seem to me to be apposite:

> We live in a time demanding change, and a time when survival is a real question. How we will succeed cannot be predicted. But we will never succeed if men of reason abdicate to those consumed by passion or by fear. Change within western nations will not come about through random acts of violence and disruption, for sheer violence cannot compel fundamental change. Rather it helps defeat those who are serious about change—the forces of humane moderation . . . Aimless and frivolous acts will turn the millions of citizens, whose fears spring from shared anxieties, frustrations and discontents, against progress and reform. Some argue that intolerance and violence are justified because modern society is violent and intolerant. Even if that were true, the argument is pure demagoguery. The objective of the

discontented should not be revenge but change. The only question for the serious man is whether these acts are effective tools of liberating change. They are not effective. They are not moral. And thus the use of violent acts is self-indulgent and, worse, the unwitting instrument of those who seek to impose oppression from the Right.

It would also in fairness be recognised that imperialisms totally without conscience do still exist. They flourish East of the Iron Curtain and East of the Urals. But violence there is futile — as nationalists in Czechoslovakia, Poland, Esthonia, Latvia, Lithuania, the Ukraine or Tibet have found. The West, for all its faults and crimes, has at least the merit that revolution against the system there is still possible.

Successful force, as an agent of political change, is dependent on persuasion also in another important sense, namely that it must persuade the population whose name is invoked of its rightness and legitimacy. The lesson of Irish history is that physical force never succeeded except when it secured the support of the Irish democracy.

The physical force movement of today differs essentially from that of fifty years ago in that it has deliberately declined to seek a mandate from the Irish people and has instead been conspicuously disavowed by the Irish electorate. For the Irish electorate is now taking a more objective view of our history and is making a more mature assessment of the meaning of the fight for freedom. The Irish people, in their great majority, now see that the purpose and the achievement of the rifles of the fight for Irish freedom were to establish the parliament and the political institutions of freedom. They see that the legitimate inheritors of the freedom-fighters now are those who strive peacefully to make these institutions, for which they fought, work towards a more just society, and who, where necessary, strive non-violently to reform those institutions so as to make Ireland more free, because more enlightened, more involved, more educated and more just.

SOLUTIONS FOR THE SEVENTIES
But freedom in Ireland, like unity and democracy, are primarily objectives which must be achieved in Ireland by Irishmen. Britain, of course, as I shall maintain later, has enormous responsibilities towards Ireland. But the solution she must work for must be an Irish solution. It must take account of the realities of two communities, two traditions, two nationalisms, two ways of being Irish — one a Republican-Irish way, one a British-Irish way. Empirical realities of the living present must guide the search for a solution — not fixed ideas left over from an abstract conception of the past.

ABSOLUTISM
The fatal weakness of the present physical-force republician tradition is that, in common with other ideologies, it imposes on empirical political facts the system-built all-purpose categories derived from an already mythologised past. In this view, people fill roles — alternately imperialist or colonist or oppressor, or republican and anti-imperialist roles — rather than being simply people. Those cast for imperialist roles are wicked and all their deeds evil; they must not be talked with or listened to. Those cast for anti-imperialist, republican or oppressed roles are virtuous and all their actions noble; but they do not need to be talked with or listened to. The imperialist does not exist as a person, only as an abstract instantiation of timeless evil. The only good imperialist is a dead one. The abstraction however takes flesh again, preferably in

what has come to be gruesomely called body-counts. It is easy to conclude: the only good Britisher is a dead one.

But this absolutist mentality has a curious boomerang effect. It sometimes seems almost as though the only good republicans were also dead ones. Our mystical republicanism of today certainly does seem to have strangely necrological leanings. One is reminded of the words of the late Father Thomas Merton, speaking about the psychological sources of war:

> In the last analysis, if there is war because nobody trusts anybody, this is because I myself am defensive, suspicious, untrusting, and intent on making other people conform themselves to my particular brand of death-wish[5].

No-one familiar with the thought of Sartre can fail to be struck by the applicability to typical representatives of the mystical-republican tradition of Sartre's devastating analysis of *l'homme serieux*, the moral fanatic of the doctrinaire Right or the ideological Left, who has all his decisions settled in advance by unarguable abstractions and all his moral judgements determined in advance by inexorable and timeless absolutes. It is morality without dialogue or discussion, without self-questioning or openness to evidence or to experience. But it is, Sartre concludes, a morality of the dead, not of the living.

But politics is morality for the living. It is patient unwearying effort to achieve obtainable good for living people now. It is open to any dialogue, ready for any discussion, with any person or group whose views are relevant or whose consent is necessary, in order that people may have peace. Without peace there will be no Ireland that either republicans or unionists will want to live in, much less enjoy the good life in. Only in peace can an Irish solution be worked out by Irishmen. It is a strange, sad fact that the two British political parties and the present British administration in the North agree with almost all Irishmen that there can be no military solution. The only people now who seem to think that a military solution is possible are extremist unionists and extremist republicans.

MILITARY SOLUTION?

A military solution is impossible. But the grim fact is that the more military methods are prolonged, the more impossible any solution will become; and, what is worse, the more impossible for any group to live in the violent society created by them will become. A policy of making the North of Ireland ungovernable will inevitably make it unbearable for Irishmen. The violence which is now practised and taught to the young as patriotism will continue, long after its motives have been forgotten. But it will then have turned to endemic and nearly ineradicable gangsterism. The danger of this increases as the tactics of the urban guerillas have to be more sporadic and probably, therefore, more reckless and more ruthless.

Sincere republicans should seriously consider whether they might come to be remembered in the future, not as the courageous freedom-fighters they earnestly intend to be, but as those who were the means—the unwilling and unwitting but nevertheless effective means — of installing permanently in Irish society the sordid, sick brutality of Al Caponism.

No-one should be so naive as to imagine that, once violence is over, normal life will simply resume again. The terrible thing about violence is that those who use it can with difficulty escape from being themselves mutilated in their persons by it. We have seen harrowing photographs of mutilated bodies, disfigured faces, people with missing limbs, from various bomb outrages. No-one can show us photographs of mutilated souls, disfigured personalities, warped consciences, especially among the young.

These wounds of the spirit may show only years afterwards in emotional and personality disturbance, antisocial behaviour, socially inadequate individual and family lives. The devastated cities and towns we can some time rebuild. But how shall we rebuild the personalities of our children, of our youth? They have had their only childhood. They will never have known a different youth. We can never offer them a second chance.

When one thinks of the long term effect of the present chapter of republican violence, one very greatly fears that one shall have to say of it in the future what Patrick Kavanagh said of his brief involvement with republicanism in his youth:

> There was no deep thought then, so profound spiritually; it was an emotional movement that left no dregs of beauty when the flood had passed.

UNIONIST VIOLENCE

To attempt to find an effective answer to republican violence, it is necessary to understand it. Understanding does not imply approval, but it does require impartial and objective appraisal.

I feel that any objective observer would have to recognise the major part played in the breeding of republican violence by official unionist policies over the past fifty years. The barricades, after all, were social, economic and political before ever they became physical. The "no-go" areas were no-industry, low-employment, no — or low — social amenity areas, areas deprived of civil rights and political equality.

It must not be forgotten now that what the world has come to know as the Catholic ghettos were deliberately created by the sectarian zoning which was the official housing policy of the Unionist Government since the State was established. These are the areas where republican violence has flourished, because these are the areas where social and political discrimination has been real and where social problems have, therefore, been most acute. In creating religious ghettos, the Unionist Government sowed dragons' teeth; is it any wonder if the first crop which has the opportunity bites?

The obviously sincere commitment of the British Secretary of State for Northern Ireland, Mr William Whitelaw, to achieving a just political solution can succeed only if he is seen to be tackling the problems of the ghettos in the ghettos. His present dilemma is that Operation Motorman will very quickly be judged by the people in the ghettos as nothing but a military imposition on them of a restored and unchanged Stormont, unless he can speedily show that the law and order they are now asked to accept is not the old "law and order and security" they have known and despised; not unionist law and Orange Order, but a genuinely new deal, and that the police force which will enforce law-keeping is not the badge of their repression but a genuinely new sort of force, creating a new kind of credibility and confidence.

TERRORISTS?

The British Secretary will have to work deliberately and quickly towards establishing, or perhaps re-establishing, his reputation for strict impartiality. The use of the term "terrorist" perhaps would provide as good a rough test as any for impartiality.

What excuse can there be any longer for reserving the term "terrorist" for the IRA and not also using it of the UDA or other "Protestant" para-military private armies, of the Tartan Gang and other "Protestant" sectarian hooligans and of Tara and other sinister sectarian killers who have already perpetrated scores of unspeakably horrible murders of Catholics, or of Protestants known to be friendly to Catholics? Until these latter groups are treated as the "terrorists" they are, and are seen to be being pursued as relentlessly and to be having their arms searched out as effectively as are the IRA, hopes of Mr Whitelaw's policies will remain dim. I do not deny that there have been brutish assassinations perpetrated by Catholics too, and some for no other reason than that their victims were Protestants. When violence gets installed in society, the life of all tends to become nasty and brutish, and the lives of too many to be tragically short.

A NEW SOCIETY
The law and order which we all, Protestants and Catholics, desperately long to see re-established, will have to be different from the unionist understanding of these in the past. There can be no return to a past of which such groups as Vanguard, UDA and the Tartans can present themselves as defenders. The only way for Northern Ireland now is forward to a new society.

There should be a regional administration in the North. No Irishman could view with anything but regret and sadness and shame the failure of what was, after all, an Irish Parliament and Government. But failure it has been and it cannot be restored, because it will not be accepted by the minority again, ever.

The new regional administration must be one radically restructured so that both communities have a genuine access to decision-making and the peace-loving majority in both communities can have a real commitment to eradicate the conditions which have favoured the bigots, the extremists, the fanatics, in their own community or evoked them in the other.

A New Ulster must be, not one made safe for unionists by more liberalism and paternalism, but one with which republicans too can identify because in it they can still identify with Ireland. It must be an Ulster accepting and welcoming the existence, within its borders, of Irish nationalism and republicanism as well as British allegience and citizenship and British or Ulster nationalism. Both conventional unionism, for which all nationalists or Catholics were by definition "disloyal", and classical republicanism for which all unionists were by definition aliens, must be seen in future as enemies of Ireland or, for those whose loyalties are British, enemies of Ulster and of Britain.

BRITAIN'S RESPONSIBILITY

I have said that the solution must be an Irish solution worked out by Irishmen. Nevertheless, Irishmen cannot work out the solution now without Britain's help. Ireland's difficulty for once is Britain's opportunity. It is not her opportunity only but her interest, nationally, politically, economically and internationally. To adapt another slogan from Ireland's patriotic past, with Ireland unpacified, Britain shall never be at peace. Britain cannot stand erect in the European Economic Community with the burden of the Irish problem around her neck. Britain cannot credibly raise her voice in protest against denials of human rights abroad, while she herself is party to their suppression in Ireland.

In the light of many events, it is surely humiliating for a Briton to read the European Convention on Human Rights, guaranteeing the right to freedom from subjection to torture, inhuman or degrading treatment or punishment; to respect for private and family life, home and correspondence; to freedom of expression, peaceful assembly and association, and to an enjoyment of all these rights without discrimination on any grounds, such as sex, race, colour, language, religion, political or other opinions, national or social origin, association with a national minority, property, birth or other status. Even when it is provided that some of these rights may be derogated from in war or public emergency, it is still expressly required that such derogations do not extend to torture or inhuman or degrading punishments.

It is important that Britain reflect on how habitually and systematically these human rights had to be abrogated over fifty years in order to maintain the Stormont regime; and on how glaringly Britain herself has had to abrogate them in the process of shoring up Stormont. In the perspective of history, Britons will have no pride or joy in the semantic rags with which Compton tried to dress up the ugly facts. She will, for many a decade, be reminded of them by oppressive regimes elsewhere, against whose injustices she tries to protest.

But Britain now has the opportunity to achieve a valid solution. There should now be no doubt that she has the will to do so. Representatives of the nationalist minority, together with political leaders in the Republic, have now a better opportunity than Ireland has ever had in fifty years to secure a fair and just settlement from Britain. It will be tragic if militant republicans are the means of losing this opportunity. It will be sad if it is in reference to them that future generations will have once more to say : "Will Ireland never get a chance?"

WHAT CAN BRITAIN DO?

The British Northern Ireland Office could be pardoned for asking what they can do next. If it is almost impossible for us Irish to know what can or should now be done, it is understandable if the British should be perplexed. The trouble with military intelligence is that it can obtain almost any information except intelligent understanding of the psychology of a population. For example, a little ordinary non-military intelligence would have kept the British Army from that gratuitous affront to nationalist sensibilities which is the occupation of Gaelic Athletic Association sports grounds by British soldiers; and from that blow to harassed parents and stress-torn children which was the occupation of schools.

Britain must take speedy steps to prove that Operation Motorman was a means not an end; was no part of a military solution but a condition of the resumption of the search for a political solution. She must visibly disassociate her security operations in all domains from any suspicion of collusion with the UDA. She must show that a political solution is and is seen to be not a restoration of the *status quo ante* but a genuinely new political deal for Ireland.

I believe that two security steps now would do more than any other to remove credibility from the IRA and deprive violence of motivation. One would be vigorous Army moves against the Protestant groups who are now defying British law and spreading panic through Catholic areas; the other the immediate release of all internees (and of the Protestant "political prisoners"). The former would, as nothing else will, convince Catholics that they do not need IRA protection. The latter would give credibility to political action by the elected representatives of the minority and at the same time deflect it from armed "defenders" of the ghettos.

ECONOMIC AID

Political action must be accompanied by economic aid. But to counteract the political thrust of unionist economic policy in the past, British economic aid now must have a calculated political thrust in a contrary, balancing direction. A few substantial factories in West Belfast would do more than exhortation and as much as political initiatives — though these too are vital — to take violence out of the Catholic ghettos. A planned policy for the industrial development of Ulster west of the Bann would have equally profound effects.

This would incidentally pay cross-community and cross-political dividends. The industrial development map of Northern Ireland can leave little doubt that the Unionist Government was deliberately building up a sort of economic "redoubt" in the North-Eastern enclave, from Craigavon to Coleraine, an area which marvellously coincided with a guaranteed and permanent unionist majority. This policy entailed the sacrificing of unionist interest in west Ulster; and this the party leaders west of the Bann seemed ready to accept with a superb — or supine — preference for ideology before bread and butter for the followers.

The selection of Derry, Enniskillen, Dungannon, Strabane, Newry, as industrial growth-centres would be welcomed, at least by west Ulster unionist workers, whatever about party leaders, no less than by nationalist workers, whose noviceship to violent protest was generations of unemployment and social deprivation. This, of course, could be done effectively only in consultation with the corresponding planning and IDA authorities in the Republic, as part of the coordinated development of the border counties on both sides of the Border. The Republic's experience in developing growth centres in Cork, Galway, Waterford, Shannon, etc., would be relevant to such a project.

It would, of course, be unfair not to point out the strong economic pull towards the Britain-ward facing East which exists in the whole island of Ireland. But the beautiful coincidence of this pull with unionist party interests meant that there was no political incentive or will to counteract economic forces for social reasons — though precisely this is a normal priority of normal modern politics.

The nationalists of the Six Counties, in whom decades of second-class citizenship have bred suspicion and cynicism, will begin to believe in a New Ulster only when they see all Ulster being developed in the interest of all Ulstermen. Naturally, therefore, such a programme of industrial development, backed up by British money, will have to be accompanied by legislation requiring all firms to have a religiously balanced work-force or to show why they have not. This should apply to existing firms as well as to ones to be established in future.

This may be thought to be, and in normal circumstances would be an unwarranted interference with personal liberty. But so much industrial enterprise is now anyhow dependent on public finance that private employers have to be prepared to accept public checks on freedom in the urgent interests of social justice and community peace. A situation brought about by decades of religious discrimination in employment can only be rectified by anti-discriminatory legislation.

UNIONISTS' CONTRIBUTION
The five months since the British initiative have been a most unhappy period for unionists. They have not enhanced the reputation of unionist party leaders.

Nationalists should not take joy from their discomfiture or try to rub salt in their wounds. Our destinies are inextricably bound up with theirs. We are tied with them to the same wheel of mutual torture — or to the same raft of common hope. We must make a sustained effort to understand their thinking and their feelings, as they must do to understand ours. We shall always have to share together this island, which each community in its own way proudly loves.

To refer to only one of the things unionists could do to understand the nationalists, it seems to me that they could try to see how unrealistic and how offensive it is for them to claim that the Republic of Ireland is a "foreign country", which has no right to "interfere" in the internal problems of Northern Ireland.

Let no-one suppose, and let no-one try to persuade either unionists or the British public, that the commitment of virtually all Irishmen in the Republic, and virtually all nationalists in the Six Counties to the reunification of Ireland is anything other than deep, earnest and ineradicable. This commitment is one of the few unchanging and unchangeable political facts of Irish life.

The Republic's view of the problem may seem at times naive and simplistic, its interest superficial and sentimental, its concern opportunistic and intermittent. But it would be a grievous error to under-estimate the commitment and a fatal political miscalculation to ignore it. The Northern problem is not an external problem for the Republic. It is an internal problem. It is by far the gravest internal problem we have. Any Irish Government which ignored this problem would have ceased to be responsible to the Irish people. It would quite simply have ceased to be responsible.

No reflection on our tradition of political violence in Ireland can ignore the fact that — apart from isolated and comparatively minor incidents of land agitation — the only cause and pretext for illegal armies and political violence in the Republic since 1922 has been the partition of Ireland. The same is true of Northern Ireland's much worse record of political violence, whether from republican or from unionist camps. Perhaps the very impasse in which reciprocal violence has now locked us may force us to be ready to explore new ways to live in peace. Perhaps "Not an inch" and "No surrender" will be looked at again, as it becomes clear that they imply "No future" and "No survival."

NATIONALISTS' CONTRIBUTION

It is easier for each community to see its virtue and the other's perfidy than for either to see its own faults. Nationalists must painstakingly try to see the intelligent and earnest unionist's point of view and to understand the less intelligent unionist's fears and prejudices. They must also seek to liberate themselves from their own shibboleths and hang-ups.

There are political risks for nationalists in talking with the "other side" or with the British Northern Ireland Office. Can these be compared to the risks to innocent life and limb and personality involved in not talking? Talking should not be made, on one side or on the other, categorically conditional on prior demands being first met. There could be logical error as well as moral fault in saying, for example, "No talks until internment ends", or "No talks until terrorism ceases", when in fact talks might be a necessary condition or a sufficient cause of the happening of either of these things.

The talks must be dominated by the passion to save lives, not to save faces. Lives can be saved only by a readiness on both sides to renounce hopes of total victory. Unionists must renounce demands for a restoration of the old Stormont, not to speak of "full integration" with Britain; nationalists must renounce hopes of a united Ireland by force or coercion ever, and hopes of a united Ireland by agreement now. If it be retorted that there is not parity between these two renunciations, I can only answer by stating my conviction that there will never be peace, for nationalists or for unionists either, in Ireland, nor peace from the Irish Problem for Britain, in any situation which is not positively open now to the prospect of an eventual Union of Ireland by mutual agreement in the future.

PROTESTANT CHURCHES' CONTRIBUTION

Despite what is sometimes thought abroad and sometimes said at home, the Northern Ireland crisis is not a religious war. It is basically a social, cultural, economic and political problem, in which religion has been exploited for political ends. It is a typically post-colonialist or post-imperialist situation with a sectarian base. That sectarian base was built for it by past British imperialist policy. It is in no spirit of rancour, and in no ploy to blame Britain for all our ills, but in strict historical objectivity, that one is compelled to say that the first people to exploit religion for political ends in Ireland were not Irishmen but British politicans.

In the past fifty years, it was not the Churches, Catholic or Protestant, which had the giving of employment, the location of industry, the allocation of houses, the controlling of electoral areas, the determining of election strategies and the concocting of political propaganda, the marshalling of votes, the distribution of benefits. But, though the Churches did not cause the problems, they could have done more and they must now do more to create conditions for a solution. The Churches enjoy immense affection and loyalty from their members. They have immense responsibility for the forming of attitudes.

Here too it is easier to see the mote in the brother's eye. I begin therefore by some remarks on the steps the Protestant Churches might take. I do this in genuine humility, trying to speak the truth, and hoping to say it in unfeigned love. I do it while praying that I will have the humility to let the truth be spoken about us to me, knowing it too to come from love.

ORANGE ORDER

If I speak first of the Orange Order, it is because what is believed to be the case in Northern Ireland is often more relevant to our present sickness than what is, but is not seen to be, the case. It is certainly believed almost universally by Catholics that the Orange Order is the great power behind unionist politics and that the Protestant Churches are heavily committed to the Orange Order. This creates among Catholics the help-less feeling that in the Orange Order they are con-fronted by a monolithic Protestant Church-State Estab-lishment, in which Protestantism comes to be thought to be the Unionist Party at prayer and the Unionist Party and the Orange Order are thought to be the Protestant Churches in parliament or on parade.

The brandishing of religious slogans on Orange banners, the preceding of political demonstrations by church parades, the presence of be-sashed Protestant clergy-men with unionist ministers of State on Orange plat-forms and among the marching ranks, the use of pro-vocative sectarian tunes, the proliferation of offensive sectarian graffiti in the Protestant streets, festooned with

Union Jacks or, more recently, with Ulster flags — all serve literally to drum home this impression.

The sectarian graffiti were at one time being condoned with a laugh as harmless folklore. But it is hardly an accident that our present troubles started in 1969 by the burning down of Catholic Bombay Street by mobs from adjacent Protestant streets, where these graffiti are particularly prolific, and are carefully renewed for every year's "Twelfth".

I believe that this noxious impression of Protestant Church-Orange Order-Unionist Party monolith can be removed only by a public decision of the Protestant Churches to withdraw from official involvement with the Orange Order. Many Protestant ministers of all Churches, with exemplary courage, have always refused to become Orangemen. Their names should be written with pride on the pages of Irish and Ulster history. But individual witness is no longer enough. An official policy of the Churches as such is needed.

PROTESTANT WITNESS

I say these things in a spirit of sincere affection for my Protestant friends in Northern Ireland. I say them only in the interests of peace and normal political life in the North. But I say them also, if I may be permitted so to put it, in the interests of Protestantism itself. Erastianism is no part of the authentic Protestant tradition. But the Church-political establishment relationship in Northern Ireland can easily look from outside to be a form of Erastianism. To disassociate themselves openly from apparent solidarity with the Unionist Party would be for the Protestant Churches a return to their genuine tradition, which is at its best an evangelically radical and prophetic tradition, and would liberate Protestantism for a more truly Protestant witness.

Ireland today needs a truly Protestant witness. The etymological and psychological root of Protestantism is protest. Some of its members and many of its friends think that Irish Protestantism has not protested enough about social injustice, about the liberty of the Christian man before the State, about the primacy of the spiritual over the political, about the claims of God as against the claims of Caesar. Protestantism in this country has perhaps invoked Romans 13:1-7 and Peter 2:13-17 too simplistically, preaching consistently that "since all government comes from God, the civil authorities were appointed by God", but perhaps preaching less insistently that "the state authorities are there to serve God for our good". Protestantism has seemed, at least to some observers, to be too concerned with not rocking the political boat, too frightened of letting the boat of the Christian Church be driven, not by changing gusts coming from the expediencies of the politicians, but by the gale-force but liberating wind of the Holy Spirit.

CATHOLIC CHURCH'S CONTRIBUTION

The beams in our Catholic eyes are more easily detected by our Protestant friends than by ourselves. If the proposed top-level meetings between Roman Catholic and Protestant Church leaders take place, I hope that we shall be looking each other in the eye and that several motes and beams can be identified on both sides, and at least some extracted. Meanwhile at least a tentative list can already be given of some of the things the Catholic Church should do.

The celebrated but pointless and meaningless article 44.2 of the Constitution, about the "special position" of the Catholic Church in the Republic should certainly have been deleted. Doubtless it helps to create the same impression among Northern Protestants of a Roman Catholic Church-State monolith, which is created for

Catholics by apparent Protestant solidarity with orange-ism and with unionism.

The case for abolition of Article 41.3.2 prohibiting divorce is surely in a quite different category. The ground stated for this prohibition in the Constitution are socio-moral, not religious or denominational. Surely there is an onus on those who propose abolition not to evade the arguments based on social morality and upon the effects of divorce legislation on society and on family stability — for these are the aspects about which the Irish electorate is worried. It is less than fair or help-ful to represent the issue solely or mainly as one of civil rights for a minority religious denomination.

The same might be said of the argument about the criminal law prohibition on contraceptive appliances, though this is not part of the Constitution. The majority of the Irish people are known to be concerned about the effects on sexual morality, especially among teenagers, of the free availability of contraceptives. No advocate of removal of the prohibition has been able to show how contraceptives can be made available without being made freely available, even to the unmarried and to adolescents. This availability would coincide with and surely massively reinforce the enormous commercial and other pressures already being exerted on our teenagers to abandon traditional restraints and values. This free availability of contraceptives the advocates of change almost certainly do not want. Quite certainly, the majority of the population of the Republic do not want it.

ECUMENISM
What undeniably is demanded of the Catholic Church at this time is a vigorous commitment to ecumenism. Not only is this necessary for the re-establishment of

community harmony and peace in Ireland at this tragic
time; not only is it therefore a matter of national survival, it is also the duty laid unequivocally upon us by
the Vatican Council. I quote from the Decree on
Ecumenism :

> (We must make) every effort to eliminate words,
> judgements and actions which do not respond to the
> conditions of separated brethren with truth and fair-
> ness and so make mutual relations between them
> more difficult. . . .

> In ecumenical work, Catholics must assuredly be
> concerned for their separated brethren, praying for
> them, keeping them informed about the Church,
> making the first approaches towards them. . . .

> Catholics must joyfully acknowledge and esteem the
> truly Christian endowments from our common heri-
> tage which are to be found among our separated
> brethren. It is right and salutary to recognise the
> riches of Christ and virtuous works in the lives of
> others who are bearing witness to Christ. . . .

> We must come to understand the outlook of our
> separated brethren. Study is absolutely required for
> this. . . .

> Of great value for this purpose are meetings between
> the two sides, especially for discussion of theological
> problems, where each can deal with the other on an
> equal footing. . . .

> Thus the way will be opened for this kind of fraternal
> rivalry to incite all to a deeper realisation and a
> clearer expression of the unfathomable riches of
> Christ. . . .

> Cooperation (in social matters) among all Christians
> vividly expresses that bond which already unites
> them, and it sets in clearer relief the features of
> Christ the Servant. Such cooperation . . . should be
> ever-increasingly developed, particularly in regions

where a social and technical evolution is taking place. It should contribute to a just appreciation of the dignity of the human person, the promotion of the blessings of peace, the application of Gospel principles to social life. . . . Christians should also work together in the use of every possible means to relieve the afflictions of our times, such as. . . . illiteracy and poverty, lack of housing, and the unequal distribution of wealth. (1. 4. 11. 9. 11. 12.)

In this spirit we must expunge from our history books and from our minds and attitudes any possibly remaining traces of older resentments against a former Ascendency. We must methodically eliminate any lurking conscious or sub-conscious tendency to rejoice in Protestant adversity or regret Protestant success. We should, for example, derive sincere joy from the building in the Republic out of public funds of Protestant schools for Protestant children. How else can Protestant witness survive in Ireland? And Ireland needs Protestant witness.

CATHOLIC SCHOOLS

On the other hand, I am convinced that the secularisation of schools in the Republic would gradually erode and finally absorb Protestant religious witness and Protestant culture. Nothing short of Hitlerian thought-control could prevent schools in most areas in the Republic from being, in any case, *de facto* Catholic, just as nothing in the Six Counties can prevent county schools from being *de facto* Protestant. What we need as national policy in the Republic and in Ireland generally, both in education and elsewhere, is genuine pluralism. . . . Pluralism is the contrary opposite of what Italians call "monocolorismo", and should, therefore, never be confused with secularism. Speaking of education, the Vatican Council has this to say about pluralism :

The state should keep in mind the principle of sub-
sidiarity so that no kind of school monopoly arises.
For such a monopoly would militate against the
native rights of the human person, the development
and spread of culture itself, the peaceful association
of citizens, and the pluralism which exists today in
very many societies. *Declaration on Christian Education, 6.*

An abuse to which Catholics must plead guilty is the
occurrence within Catholic churches or their precincts
of para-military manifestations at funerals. Such manifestations (I am not now referring to the traditional
ceremonial for official State funerals) introduce into the
Church elements and emotions totally repugnant to the
Christian liturgy of death. They convey to Protestants
the deplorable and utterly false impression that Catholic
priests are supporting and blessing the IRA. The Christian faith and conscience of our people should be
enough to show them that such displays have no place
in the house of God, which is a house of peace and love,
the house of him who prayed to the Father : "May
they all be one."

THE REPUBLIC'S POLITICAL ASSETS

The new Ireland should be a synthesis of what is best
in the two Irish cultures, the two Irish religions and
national traditions. The tension between them can
be creative. Both parts of Ireland will remain the poorer
until their creative symbiosis is restored. In the Republic
we have defects and shortcomings, and indeed compare
unfavourably in certain respects with the North. But
in the matter of political sectarianism, the record of the
Republic is a proud and noble one. I doubt if any ex-
colonial regime, after a war of national liberation, can
parallel free Ireland's instant and systematic repudiation of revanchism against the representatives of the

former colonial power, or can rival Ireland's systematic tolerance and generosity towards its religious minority. Sectarianism is not and never was an issue in the Irish Republic's political tradition. Social and political ecumenism is a spontaneous trait of the Irish character.

But what the Republic does need to rethink is its nationalistic ritual of commemorative glorification of violent revolution. It is this which at times created an ugly ambivalence in public attitudes towards violence in the North. It helps to perpetuate a sense of siege and stockade among Northern Protestants. It continues to make it more difficult for young people to form a positive and constructive concept of patriotism.

We need to launch a determined multi-media programme to educate our people away from the romantic myth of nationalistic and revolutionary violence. A very significant contribution could be made to pacification with justice in Ireland now by an agreed decision by 1916-1922 veterans and all political parties and public bodies in the Republic to abstain from all commemorative parades for at least a five or ten year period.

This would be tangible evidence that we are no longer hugging our memories of the Old Ireland, but have our faces set towards a new one. This would be true fidelity to the spirit of the men who fought and died for Ireland. For they fought and died solely to achieve for us free and democratic institutions, in order that we might use them to build the just and enlightened and compassionate Ireland of the Democratic Programme. We honour their memory by using these institutions to create a New Ireland. For the New Ireland is in our own hands now; and the tools needed for shaping it now are no longer rifles.

THE NORTHERN IRISHMAN'S CONTRIBUTION

We can learn much in its shaping from our fellow-Irishmen in the North. The trouble in the North is not the people, not their church loyalties, not their educational nor their social system; the trouble is simply their politics. It is unfortunate that no society can in the long run be better than its politics — for most other things created by Protestants in the North are admirable. Northern Protestants are a sturdy, manly, honest, industrious, shrewd, loyal and lovable people. As people, as Ulstermen, as Irishmen, they share the qualities of our own Monaghan, Cavan and Donegal men : for the best qualities of Ulster regionalism do not stop at the border on either side.

For a people officially and deeply committed to reunification of this island, we in the Republic have made surprisingly little effort to know and to understand the Northern people. That is our loss. It is a curious paradox that the key people in most of the relevant departments in the Republic probably know more about the social services, the educational and health services, the university situation, the road and communications systems in England than about those in the North of Ireland.

Almost certainly, more is known in university circles in the Republic about English universities than about Queen's University, Belfast, or the New University of Ulster in Coleraine. Yet few universities in these islands have so much to teach us in this time of explosion in third-level education as Queen's, about university expansion, administration, staff-student relations, student self-government and student-participation in administration. Queen's University's success in maintaining, through these bitter years of violence, not only a balanced but a courageously liberal stance, deserves to be studied by other sectors of society in Ireland, North and South.

Northern Ireland's social, educational, youth, health and rural services, and young offender services, deserve attentive study from all who are concerned with social progress in the Republic. Northern Ireland's Civil Service is characterised by courtesy, efficiency, and fair-mindedness. The laws given them by politicians to administer are not always fair; but they administer them fairly. And all this is happening in our own country two hours' journey from Dublin. It all helps to show what we lost when the Six Counties were cut off; just as the present horrible sickness of their society shows what the Northern unionists lost when they cut themselves off from us. It is sometimes said that Ireland is too small to be able to afford two administrations. What certainly is true is that Ireland cannot afford two administrations unless the complementary qualities and skills of both are somehow made available to the whole island.

POLITICAL RENEWAL IN THE REPUBLIC

Both parts of Ireland badly need a new start. The present crisis in the North could be purgative and purifying if it forced both communities and their respective political parties into searching self-examination and renewal. For politics and politicians in the Republic, the North should now be seen as a moral challenge.

Political parties must, faced with the debacle in the North, try to make sure that nothing in party cumainn ever resembles, even distantly, the secret deals, the hidden pressures, the "jobs for the brethren" methods we associate rightly or wrongly, with the Orange Lodge in the North.

No society can ultimately be better than its politics. Renewal of politics is an urgent need in Ireland now. We need greater respect for politics and politicians, greater esteem for political life. This, I believe, is not withheld when politicians are seen to deserve it. We need more, not fewer, full-time politicians, professionally concerned about the nation's problems and the public good, and not just about voters' pension awards or social benefits, which anyhow are or should be automatically guaranteed by law.

The need is scarcely for a new political party, but rather for new thinking, new methods, new men in the existing parties. Putting it cynically, one could say that the existing parties are too strong for political renewal to happen outside them — they could always stifle it. More hopefully and more fairly, one can say that there is sufficient awareness of the country's need at this time of historic decision in Ireland to give good hope that renewal will come from within the parties.

MASS MEDIA

A further major help towards and at the same time a further challenge to the renewal of politics in this country is the advent of television, together with the increasingly vigilant role towards our national institutions and way of life adopted by radio and the press. It is a role with a venerable tradition. Socrates called himself the gad-fly to the democracy. Democracy does not like gad-flies; but it needs them. A free, independent, informed, socially conscious and morally responsible press, radio and television are now indispensible safe-guards in modern democracy.

I believe that the first bell for the passing of the old Stormont was tolled years ago by the advent of television. Malcolm Muggeridge said recently in criticism of television that since its introduction it had become impossible for any modern State ever again to win a war or to suppress a revolution. If one reads "non-violent and just social protest" for "revolution", one could perhaps turn these words into a deserved tribute to television.

With occasional regrettable lapses into vulgarity—all the more tiresome because so obviously showing the hand of provincials cogging from the less reputable sections of the "metropolitan", i.e. British, media — the press, together with radio and television in Ireland have contributed to the growing awareness, greater social consciousness, wider information and increased maturity and tolerance of Irish people on both sides of the Border.

The responsibility of media communicators is great, their need for moral responsibility and integrity enormous. One of the problems of democracy is to devise acceptable ways of reconciling their responsibility to society with their necessary freedom. One of the few things which is certain in this domain is that the one form of control which is worse than no control is political control. There are dangers in free media; any responsible society must take steps to cope with them. But the dangers of unfree media are greater. These dangers take longer to show; but the damage has always a long start before the symptoms appear.

THE FUTURE

The very gravity and even apparent hopelessness of the hour in Ireland can be a motive for truly Christian confidence; for Christian hope "against hope believes in hope". President Kennedy said in Dublin in 1963 :

The supreme reality of our time is our indivisibility

as children of God and our common vulnerability on this planet.

Change "planet" to "island", and we have a remarkably apt description of our situation as Catholics and Protestants in Ireland now. The deep Christian faith which characterises all religious denominations in Ireland offers us sure grounds for hope. In our common allegiance to one Lord, the Prince of Peace, whose one Commandment was "Love one another", we Christians must together find the answer to the men of hate and violence.

This common Christian witness must find expression in a common dedication by all Christians to the building up of structures of justice and harmony in our society. The Christian command of love our neighbour includes the command to reform the conditions which deny love to our neighbour and to create the institutions and structures in which love can be effective.

The choice in Ireland now lies between Christian charity and justice on one hand and insane self-destruction of the Irish nation on the other. The only liveable future for Ireland lies in the man of Christian charity. As Pope John XXIII said, the man of christian charity alone is a creator of peace :

> (He) will follow his path, lighting the lamps of joy and playing their brilliance and loveliness on the hearts of men across the surface of the globe, leading them to recognise across all borders the faces of their brothers, the faces of their friends.

Part Three

Christ and the Irish Crisis

Rationalise or theologise about it how we will, the words of Christ on violence are plain and clear. The example of Christ in regard to violence and men of violence is unmistakable.

Christ and the Irish Crisis

Address at an Interdenominational Service of Prayer for Peace and Reconciliation in Ireland held in the Methodist Central Hall, Westminster, May 24th, 1972. The address was published in The Furrow *(July, 1972) and is reprinted here by kind permission of the Editor.*

There is only one final answer to any human problem, and it is Christ. His Spirit, his love, his justice, alone are adequate response to the aspiration and anguish of mankind. The only question worth asking for all of us Christians gathered here this evening is: "What does Christ say to our situation in Ireland today? What does his Spirit say to the Churches in the North of Ireland now?"

A Christian would indeed be faithless and perverse if he did not feel that Christ's message to Ireland now is the same as when he first began to proclaim the kingdom: "Repent and believe the Gospel." We all have much to repent of — for the complacency, the lack of moral courage, the inertia, with which we have tolerated for fifty years a situation which, every fifteen of those years, on average, has erupted in communal violence, and which now, at last, has us all caught helplessly in the grip of a chronic infection of violence, from which it seems humanly almost impossible to shake ourselves free.

We have to repent of our failure to have the courage to love, which is simply another name for our failure to have the strength to be Christian. In other words, we have to repent of our failure to believe the Gospel. For to believe the Gospel is above all to believe in love — where love is not a warm glow of individualist senti- ment but is also the fulfilment of the law of justice and must therefore be embodied in just laws and just social structures. God is love; God is just; and there is only one God. Thomas Jefferson said : "I tremble for my country when I reflect that God is just."

CHRIST'S EXAMPLE

Rationalise or theologise about it how we will, the words of Christ on violence are plain and clear, the example of Christ in regard to violence and men of violence is unmistakable. His intimate circle of the twelve included several ex-freedom-fighters for Israel, one of them always still called Simon the Zealot. But it included also the ex-quisling, Matthew, the publican. It wasn't easy for them to love one another — no easier than for Ulster loyalist and Irish republican. Yet this was the community Jesus gradually, patiently, coaxed into being a community of love, a band of brothers.

The Jews too knew of no-go areas, which no loyal Israelite would willingly enter or even be allowed to enter. Samaria was such an area.

Samaritans were people no right-thinking Jew would easily feel himself expected to love. Yet Samaritans were precisely the example Jesus chose to illustrate his teaching on love. We can sense in the gospels something of the backlash of the Jews against Christ's teaching on charity towards the Samaritans. One can still picture even good and pious Jews saying : "Love is all right, up to a certain point, but you have to draw the line somewhere." For, as St John drily remarks, "Jews in fact do not associate with Samaritans."

The holy hatred of the Jews for the impossible Samaritans was thoroughly reciprocated. Each people felt entirely innocent, and even patriotically loyal and religiously righteous in their resentfulness and suspicion towards the other. Each was convinced of being thoroughly justified in refusing any sort of dialogue with the other. Simply to be a Jew was enough to be boycotted in Samaria and vice-versa.

On one occasion, Jesus himself and the disciples were passing through Samaria, and were refused admission to a village there, for no other reason, St Luke points out, but that Jesus was making for Jerusalem. John and James, the fiery ones—our Lord called them Boanerges, "the sons of thunder", or, as we might say, the hardliners; perhaps even, according to our allegiances, the UDA or the IRA supporters — thought that "fire from heaven to burn them up" was no more than these villagers deserved.

If we blame them, let us just think for a moment of the emotional reactions we have had to repeated outrages over the past three years, and how our reactions varied according to whether it was "our side" or "the other side" which suffered. After all, the insult to their gentle and beloved Master was more than flesh and blood could bear. But Jesus would have none of it. "He turned and rebuked them." He said : "You do not know of what spirit you are."

The story has two sequels. The first is that the John in question, after he had seen on Calvary what the message of Christ really meant, after he had lived for years in the memory of Christ's life and words and in the daily experience of Christ's presence in the Church and in the Eucharist, and after he had lived for years in the company of Christ's mother, came to the point where, in his old age, he could only preach one sermon and ever repeat only one thing: "Little children, love one another", and when they grumbled: "Not that . . . again!" he would answer: "But that's the whole of the Master's teaching, and nothing else is needed."

The second sequel is that the next time Samaria is mentioned in the New Testament it is in the Acts of the Apostles, where we read that the whole population of a town in Samaria "united in welcoming the message Philip preached" to them about Christ, "and as a result there was great rejoicing in that town". It could have been the very same town that John and James had wanted blown up. If the burners and bombers had had their way Jesus would have been denied the love of the people of that town.

There is something of the "son of thunder", the hard-liner, in every one of us. Do we know of what spirit we are? If it is the spirit of hate and revenge, then we are not of the spirit of Jesus. We are not true to the Holy Spirit of Jesus that we received at our baptism.

THE BOND OF BAPTISM

The fact of our common baptism in Christ is the most total condemnation of all the wrongs we have done or have allowed to happen, or simply have not noticed happening in Ireland for the last fifty years. For baptism is our common commitment to a life-style based on charity, charity first, last and always, charity when it costs, charity till it hurts, charity when it's crucifying. "My love," a saint said, "is crucified."

Baptism is a complete condemnation of sectarianism. One of the first Christian sermons, preached by St Peter, began with the words: "The truth I have come to realise is that God does not have favourites." All that are baptised in Christ are equally God's favourites.

Baptism is the indictment of all our divisive attitudes and discriminatory practices, our elitism and social or class or community superiorities. To be God's son by baptism should be more important to us than to be a unionist's son or a nationalist's son. It should not matter to us whose brother a man is, or to what brother-hood, orange or green, he belongs, when each man is Christ's brother. In the beautiful old medieval English phrase, every man is my equal, my "even Christian".

To see Christ in others, love him and serve him in others, that is faith in action, faith proved authentic. To despise, insult, hurt or hate others is to do just that to Christ. These are ways of betraying the faith.

St James says it : "My brothers, do not try to combine faith in Jesus Christ, our glorified Lord, with the mak-ing of distinctions between classes of people." (*James* 2:1.) St John says: "Anyone who says 'I love God' and hates his brother is a liar." (1 *John* 4:20.) These two, remember, were the very two "sons of thunder" who wanted to burn out the Samaritans.

DARKNESS AND LIGHT
Our Lord, as reported by St John in his gospel, says :

> The light will be with you only a little longer now.
> Walk while you have the light,
> or the dark will overtake you;
> he who walks in the dark does not know where he
>   is going.
> While you still have the light,
> believe in the light
> and you will become sons of light (*John* 12 :35-6).

St John, the disciple so close to the heart of Christ that

he is simply called "the disciple", writes in his own epistle :

> Anyone who loves his brother is living in the light
> and need not be afraid of stumbling :
> unlike the man who hates his brother and is in the
>   darkness,
> not knowing where he is going
> because it is too dark to see (1 *John* 2 :9-11).

It is a fundamental part of Christian teaching that the test of true faith is charity. Our faith, says St Paul, is a faith that works by love. For St John, as well as for St James, there are two ways of denying God, two forms of atheism : one is apostasy or deliberate rejection of the true faith; the other is refusal to love. God is love. The New Testament message is that we believe in God by affirming that he exists and by manifesting our belief through the love we show in our behaviour. To deny love to God's beloved children is to deny God himself who is love.

For St John there are two ways of coming to the light which is Christ. One is to believe in him by accepting Christian truth, the other is to love his brothers. These two ways are inseparable. For the same St John there are two ways of walking away from the light of Christ into the darkness of disbelief. One is to deny that Christ is God. The other is to refuse to love Christ's brothers; for this is to deny that the Father is love and that Christ is the gift of his love to men. And these two ways of darkness are inseparable. What a need we Irish have to pray: "God, enlighten our darkness"!

VIOLENCE AND NON-VIOLENCE

One trouble with Christian preaching on love is that it can so easily sink into the pleasant analgesic glow of sentimental moralising. The realist will say it is utopian; the marxist simply calls it opium. But it does work. It is the man who asks how many battalions the Church has who goes down disgraced to his unhonoured grave. Non-violence, despite the propagandists of the militarist power-complexes and the revolutionary theoreticians, does work. It has done more for human progress than violence has ever done. No war-lord, no captain of revolutionary violence, has ever shaped history as Christ's message of love has shaped it — despite the hardness of arteries and heart of so many of Christ's supposed followers. Gandhi will still speak when the guns from Bangla Desh to Derry are silent. Martin Luther King was not silenced when the bigot's gun had done; who remembers now his assassin's name?

In Ireland, we have, on both sides, too exclusively honoured our men of the rifle, too little remembered our men of peace and reconciliation. But our O'Connells, our Davitts, our Parnells, served Ireland as bravely and as nobly as our Sarsfields, our Pearses and our Michael Collinses. In the North, our Sharman Crawfords, our Rev. J. B. Armours and our Robert Hicksons served Ulster as honourably and as valiantly as our Carsons.

Martin Luther King said :

> Violence brings only temporary victories; violence, by creating many more social problems than it solves, never brings permanent peace. I am convinced that if we succumb to the temptation to use violence in our struggle for freedom, unborn generations will be the recipients of a long and desolate night of bitterness, and our chief legacy to them will be a never-ending reign of chaos[6].

He could say the same thing to our gunmen and bombers on both sides in the North of Ireland today.

But surely three hundred dead, a hundred million pounds' worth of destruction are enough. May the dead not have lived in vain. Catholic and Protestant, Irish and English, loyalist and republican, they are now together in the loving mercy of their common Lord and brother, Christ. May he have mercy on the living and grant us peace.

Lady Gregory wrote a poem about the Irish 1916, "An Old Woman Remembers." It ends:

> Yet who forgives shall be forgiven;
> It's likely in the shining land,
> When near the company of heaven
> The wondering shadow-armies stand,
> The barren shadow-weapons fall,
> The bitter battle-angers cease;
> So may God give them and all
> The blessing of his lasting peace!

I think I can voice the feelings of us all in the prayer of Azariah from the book of Daniel:

> Lord, now we are the least of all the nations,
> now we are despised throughout the world, today,
>   because of our sins.
> We have at this time no leader, no prophet, no prince,
>   no holocaust,
> no sacrifice, no oblation, no incense,
> no place where we can offer you the first-fruits,
> and win your favour.
> But may the contrite soul, the humbled spirit be
>   acceptable to you
> and may it be your will that we follow you whole-
>   heartedly,
> since those who put their trust in you will not be
>   disappointed.
> And now we put our whole heart into following you,
> into fearing you and seeking your face once more.
> Do not disappoint us;
> treat us gently, as you yourself are gentle
> and very merciful.

Grant us deliverance worthy of your wonderful deeds,
let your name win glory, Lord (*Daniel* 3 :37-45).

The Way of the Cross
in Ireland now

A sermon preached at the dedication of the new Church of the Way of the Cross, Togher, Cork, on July 29th, 1972.

T. S. Elliot, in his poetic drama *The Rock,* after describing the dedication of a church, asks the question :

> And what shall we say of the future? Is one church all we can build?
> Or shall the visible Church go on to conquer the world?

To be true to Christ's message and mandate, we must always see our task as being to "go on to conquer the world". But how?

To this question there can be no answer except that already given by the New Testament. What alone can conquer the world is the power of our faith and the power of the Cross; and these two are one and the same power. Listen to St John :

> This is the victory over the world —
> our faith.
> Who can overcome the World?
> Only the man who believes that Jesus is the Son of God (1 *John* 5 : 4-5).

Listen to St Paul :

> While the Jews demand miracles and the Greeks

look for wisdom, here are we preaching a crucified
Christ; to the Jews an obstacle that they cannot get
over, to the pagans madness, but to those who have
been called, whether they are Jews or Greeks, a
Christ who is the power and the wisdom of God. For
God's foolishness is wiser than human wisdom, and
God's weakness is stronger than human strength . . .
During my stay with you, the only knowledge I
claimed to have was about Jesus, and only about him
as the crucified Christ. . . . In my speeches and the
sermons that I gave, there were none of the arguments that belong to philosophy; only a demonstra-
tion of the power of the Spirit. And I did this so that
your faith should not depend on human philosophy
but on the power of God (1 *Corinthians* 1:22-25;
2:2-5).

It was not triumphalism, but their certitude that true
triumph comes only from the crucified Christ, that
inspired the early Christians, after Constantine, to erect
the Cross over the palaces that were the glory of the
Caesars and over the temples of their gods that failed.
We always need to be reminded of that message; the
victory of Christ is never a military victory, never
merely a political land-slide, never just a national or
even a social revolution.

True Christian victory over the world lies only through
suffering with Christ, the Man of Sorrows, the King
whose Kingdom is not of this world. Christ himself said
to the two disciples on the way to Emmaus, after the
Resurrection :

Was it not ordained that the Christ should suffer and
so enter into his glory?

But we, his disciples of today, still find it hard to accept
this message, still need his rebuke :

You foolish men ! So slow to believe the full message
of the prophets! (*Luke* 24 : 25-26).

It is important that we should see the devotion of the Way of the Cross, not just as devotion apart from, or added on to, or even side by side with, our daily life; but to see it as entering into the very texture of our daily life.

We must always remember that Christ is not a distant Figure, who lived in a far-away country in a different culture, two thousand years ago; and not even only as the Risen Lord who lives in an "other" Kingdom in "another" heavenly world. We must always see Christ as God-with-us now and here.

Christ is the Great Contemporary, the only true contemporary. As we say in the Easter Liturgy, "all time belongs to him and all the ages". All ages and generations, all climates and cultures, are equidistant from him. The Cross of Christ is truly the centre of the universe and of human history.

Christ chose to enter fully into our history and to share completely in every dimension of human experience. He chose that there should be no situation in our lives and in our history, that there should not be a single one of "the joys and the hopes, the griefs and the anxieties of the men of this age, especially those who are poor or in any way afflicted" (*Gaudium et Spes* 1), of which we would not be able to say : "Christ shares this with us; Christ is with us through this."

In the Prologue of St John's gospel we find the words which are so familiar to us from our daily Angelus:

The Word was made flesh,
He lived among us (*John* 1 :14).

The words have a deeper meaning than appears in our English translation. Really they mean, "He pitched his tent among us." Here in turn there are two levels of

meaning. Among nomadic people, — and we are all
the Pilgrim People of God, constantly on the march
through life and through history until we come to the
Promised Land which our Lord has prepared for us —
to "pitch one's tent" with a group of people was to
"throw one's lot in" with them, to be willing to share,
for better or worse, their problems and their struggles,
their successes and their failures. This is what Christ
was willing to do for us.

There is also a deeper level of meaning here. The Tent,
otherwise called the Tabernacle, in the Bible is always
the place where God, in all his glory, power and
majesty, lives among his people, moving with them
wherever they move, constantly available to them to
listen to their prayers, shelter them with his love,
strengthen them in trial, support them by his power. In
the New Testament it is always Christ himself who,
through the Incarnation, the Passion and the Resurrection, is the true and only Tent or Tabernacle where
God forever dwells among his people. He and he alone
makes it possible for men to share the life of God,
because in him God has first shared the life of men.

He is the meeting place between God and men; he,
who is truly God, entered human experience in order
that, through him, all human experience might be
lifted up to God. Christ fully reconciles man with God,
and makes it possible for man in every situation and
experience to encounter God, through his own total
and unconditional obedience to his Father in every
experience and in every situation of his own human
life. The Letter to the Hebrews tells us : "although he
was Son, he learnt obedience through suffering" (*Hebrews* 5 :7).

Believing in Christ for us means our total identification

with him. Faith is our unconditional commitment to throw in our lot with him who chose to throw in his lot with us. This must entail our readiness to imitate in all things and in all circumstances his obedience to the Father's Will. This obedience must, for us as for Christ himself, entail suffering. St Paul speaks repeatedly of "the obedience of faith". This obedience has to be learned by us through suffering.

THIS IS THE LAMB OF GOD

In the very first chapter of St John's gospel, immediately after the Prologue, we find the first statement of the Christian faith, the very first formulation of the Christian Creed. It comes in the form of St John the Baptist's words: "Look, there is the Lamb of God that takes away the sins of the world" (*John* 1:29). We still make our affirmation of our faith in exactly the same words every day, immediately before Communion at Mass. The whole theology of the Cross and the Redemption of mankind through the Cross is contained in these words.

The words themselves are a summary of "the full message of the prophets", to which Christ referred the two disciples on the Emmaus road. They refer especially to the teaching about the coming Messiah as the Suffering Servant of God, which we find in the Prophet Isaiah; and, in particular, to that chapter of Isaiah which is called "the fourth song of the servant of the Lord". The words are familiar; but when words are too familiar we tend to "switch off", and not really to listen. We need deliberately to bring ourselves to attention in order to listen to the Bible's message.

> The crowds were appalled on seeing him
> — so disfigured did he look
> that he seemed no longer human . . .

Without beauty, without majesty (we saw him),
no looks to attract our eyes;
a thing despised and rejected by men,
a man of sorrows and familiar with suffering,
a man to make people screen their faces;
he was despised and we took no account of him.
And yet ours were the sufferings he bore,
ours the sorrows he carried.
But we, we thought of him as someone punished,
struck by God, and brought low.
Yet he was pierced through for our faults,
crushed for our sins.
On him lies a punishment that brings us peace,
and through his wounds we are healed.
We had all gone astray like sheep,
each taking his own way,
and the Lord burdened him
with the sins of all of us.
Harshly dealt with, he bore it humbly,
he never opened his mouth,
like a lamb that is led to the slaughter-house,
like a sheep that is dumb before its shearers
never opening its mouth. . . .
By his suffering shall my servant justify many,
taking their faults on himself. . . .
while he was bearing the faults of many
and praying all the time for sinners
(*Isaiah* 52:14; 53:12).

Here we have Christ's Way of the Cross vividly des-
cribed in all its tragic realism, six hundred years at
least before it happened. But we must see it again with
equal vividness and realism, two thousand years after
it happened, as a reality of our time and of our experience.

CHRIST AND THE SICK
Sickness, pain and suffering, whether in our own lives
or in the lives of those around us, and especially those

we love, are an inescapable part of the experience of all of us. We know the part that the priest plays in our times of suffering and of illness. His personal comforting, and above all the comforting of Christ which he brings us through the sacraments, make the burden less crushing and help us to be less afraid.

The priest, for his part, never feels more a priest of Christ than when he is bending over the bed of sickness — except, of course, when he is standing at the altar where, in his hands, the world's greatest love is sealed in Christ's blood, and the concentrated suffering of the world is sanctified in the "Body given up for us and for all men so that sins may be forgiven". The priest, in Christ's name, loves to comfort; but, having comforted, he walks away in his health and leaves the sick man in his pain. Would he be willing, would I be willing, would you be willing, if it were in our power, to change places with the sick man, the disfigured man, the paralysed man, the incurable man?

But this is what Christ did. He not only comforts the suffering and passes on. He becomes himself one of the sufferers. Having the power, and with full freedom, by deliberate choice, he elected to change places with the disfigured, the maimed, the men doomed to die. St John tells us :

No-one takes (my life) from me;
I lay it down of my own free will,
and it is in my power to lay it down (*John* 10 :17-18).

We are frightened at the thought of suffering in our own persons or at the sight of suffering in others. The sight of blood, the thought of a traffic accident, the fear of bodily dismemberment, makes cowards of the strongest of us. Even the thought of the dentist's chair makes brave men wilt. But of Christ we read in Isaiah :

The crowds were appalled on seeing him
— so disfigured did he look
that he seemed no longer human . . .
he was despised and we took no account of him.

We are familiar through these tragic years in Ireland
with descriptions, or even photographs, of people
mutilated by bombs, gashed by flying glass, left eyeless
from rubber bullets, maimed for life by bombs. A man
or a woman facially disfigured will undergo years of
plastic surgery in the attempt to have looks and beauty
restored. But Christ chose, not just to be someone who
would care for and nurse and comfort the victims of
violence; he became himself the victim of violence. Let
us read further from Isaiah :

Without beauty, without majesty (we saw him),
no looks to attract our eyes;
a thing despised and rejected by men . . .
a man to make people screen their faces.

CHRIST AND THE OPPRESSED

We have been familiar throughout our history with
oppression and repudiation of people by the "forces of
law and order", against which there was no appeal to
the claims of justice. We have become familiar again,
in these recent terrible times in the North, with the
abuse of power to crush human rights and liberties.

We have seen husbands, fathers, bread-winners, sons,
fiances, bundled in the night into military trucks and
hauled off to internment without trial, leaving behind
them weeping wives and terrified children in their
ransacked homes. We have read of men subjected to the
crudest forms of physical brutality and the most sophis-
ticated modes of mental torture, without being allowed
to say a word in their own defence. We have read of
men and girls and women abducted, beaten, tortured by

republicans to whom guns gave temporary power to intimidate their neighbours. Their victims too had no-one to plead their defence, no voice to assert the rights of justice against the power of guns. Those who were only tarred and feathered were the lucky ones. Others, without warning, without priest, without prayer, were shot through the head, instantly, brutally dead. The UDA have done and are doing the same.

The bullets of the one side as of the other have no political labels; just as the tears at the gravesides of both sets of victims have no colour. In pain and in grief, in death and in bereavement, we are not political enemies, we are only men. We are not republicans or unionists, we are only poor common weeping human beings.

And Christ is there to share our sorrow. He is not there to speak words of comfort. He is not there even only as a mourner. He is there as one of the innocent victims of oppression, intimidation, heartless violence. Let us read Isaiah :

> By force and by law he was taken;
> would anyone plead his cause?
> Yes, he was torn away from the land of the living!
> For our faults struck down in death.
> They gave him a grave with the wicked,
> though he had done no wrong
> and there had been no perjury in his mouth
> (*Isaiah* 53 : 8-8).

CHRIST AND THE INSULTED

We have known, in these recent brutal years in our country, of people subjected to the most vile and vicious language of vulgarity and insult, whether coming from soldiers or from sectarian mobs. When we read of degrading torture, intimidation, verbal violence, let us recall the Passion of our Lord :

At the high priest's house, the men who guarded Jesus were mocking and beating him. They blindfolded him and questioned him. "Play the prophet", they said. "Who hit you then?" And they continued heaping insults on him (*Luke* 22 :63-65).

The governor's soldiers took Jesus with them into the Praetorium and collected the whole cohort round him. Then they stripped him and made him wear a scarlet cloak, and having twisted some thorns into a crown they put this on his head and placed a reed in his right hand. To make fun of him they knelt to him saying: "Hail, king of the Jews!" And they spat on him and took the reed and struck him on the head with it (*Matthew* 27 :27-30).

They dressed him up in purple, twisted some thorns into a crown and put it on him. And they began saluting him: "Hail, King of the Jews!" They struck his head with a reed and spat on him; and they went down on their knees to do him homage (*Mark* 15 :16-19). And when they had finished making fun of him they took off the purple and dressed him in his own clothes (*Mark* 15 :16-20). (Before Herod) the chief priest and the scribes were there, violently pressing their accusations. Then Herod, together with his guards, treated him with contempt and made fun of him; he put a rich cloak on him and sent him back to Pilate (*Luke* 23 :8-11).

Pilate had Jesus taken away and scourged; and after this, the soldiers twisted some thorns into a crown and put it on his head and dressed him in a purple robe. They kept coming up to him saying: "Hail, King of the Jews!"; and they slapped him in the face (*John* 19 :1-3).

And in all this, as Isaiah said :

Harshly dealt with, he bore it humbly,
he never opened his mouth,

like a lamb that is led to the slaughter-house,
like a sheep that is dumb before its shearers,
never opening its mouth (*Isaiah* 53 : 7).

As the Gospel accounts of the Passion tell us :

When he was accused by the chief priests and the
elders he refused to answer at all ... To the governor's
complete amazement, he offered no reply to any of
the charges (*Matthew* 27 :11-14).

Jesus did not make speeches against violence : he denounced it by becoming its silent, unprotesting and
forgiving victim. Christ's Cross will stand for all time
as the condemnation of man's violence to his fellow-
man, which is only the continuation throughout history
of man's insulting and torturing of Christ's members.
And from the Cross there goes up for all time to the
Father Christ's prayer :

Father, forgive them; they do not know what they
are doing (*Luke* 23 :33-34).

PAIN WITHOUT ANAESTHETIC

Christ having full power to escape it, of his own
deliberate choice and out of sheer and unreturned love,
elected to drink the cup of human sorrow right to the
bitter dregs. There was no refinement of human
cruelty, no twist of human pain, no fear, anxiety or
desolation of the human spirit, no sense of human failure
or shame, that Christ did not will to share in his own
soul and body. There was no chloroform at the Passion.
There were no anaesthetics, no pain-killing drugs, no
sedatives, no tranquillisers. There were many to jeer in
contempt; few, very few, to sympathise or offer comfort.

Not but what anaesthetics were offered to him, in the
only form known at the time. The Roman soldiers were
not, we should remember, particularly cruel. They

were only doing the job for which they were paid. They did have hearts beneath their iron breastplates. And they did have pity for this particular victim, who was so strangely different from anyone they had ever been asked to "do a job on" before. We read :

> When they had reached a place called Golgotha, they gave him wine to drink mixed with gall, which he tasted but refused to drink (*Matthew* 27 :32-34).

In fact, what the soldiers were offering him was the only equivalent they knew of a pain-killing potion; and in their rough pity they wanted to try to lessen for him the atrocious pain of the nailing and the crucifying that was now to follow. But Jesus would not drink. He did not want to be spared one spasm of the pain. He wanted to concentrate into his Passion all the anguish and all the agony of the world, in order that all men in all time might know that in their pain he was their fellow-sufferer.

DEATH WITHOUT DIGNITY

For us the Passion is holy and our devotion has surrounded the scene on the Cross with reverence and divine dignity. But the actual Cross of Christ was for those who saw it happen death without dignity, death in disgrace and degradation.

> The passers-by jeered at him . . . the chief priests with the scribes and elders mocked him in the same way. . . . Even the robbers who were crucified with him taunted him in the same way (*Matthew* 27 :39-46).

For us, the Cross itself is the sacred emblem of our faith, the symbol of all that we value most in life and in death. For Christ, the Cross was a mark of shame and religious defilement. It marked anyone who died on it as accursed, unworthy to stand on the sacred soil of the holy city of

Sion. Anyone who even touched the cross of crucifixion was *ipso facto* defiled and needed ritual purification before he could even pray again among the holy people of God. The Law said:

> The one who has been hanged on a tree is accursed of God and you must not defile the land that the Lord your God gives you for an inheritance (*Deuteronomy* 21:23).

Jesus in his human religious psychology had the instinctive feelings and reactions of the devout Jew. He felt in all his being this revulsion from the shame and uncleanness of the Cross. He accepted this repulsive contagion for our sake, so that even in the depths of shame he could feel and be one of us.

The religious disgrace and defilement of crucifixion was such that it had by law to be carried out outside the gates of the Holy City, so that the holy enclosure within the walls of God's city might not be made impure by it. Christ endured to be treated as one impure, as one unfit to die within the Holy City. He was pushed and dragged to death outside the city walls. Yet it was his Father's city. Yet he was the Holy One of God. We must be ready, St Paul says, to join him there, in his shame, outside the walls.

> Let us not lose sight of Jesus. . . . He endured the Cross, disregarding the shamefulness of it. . . . He suffered outside the gate, to sanctify the people with his own blood. Let us go out to him then, outside the camp, and share his degradation (*Hebrews* 12:2; 13:12-13).

For he suffered this, suffered there, precisely in order to share even degrading suffering with us. And since man's inhumanity to man throughout history would contain so much sadistic urge not only to inflict pain but to insult and humiliate and dehumanise the victim, Christ freely accepted this way to suffer in order to be for all time on the side of the sufferer, in order to be

> capable of feeling all our weaknesses with us and to be . . . tried in every way that we are, though he is without sin (*Hebrews* 4 :15).

He suffered in this way precisely in order that when we suffered humiliation, shame, disgrace and failure, we might know that in and by that kind of suffering we were being lifted up to where he is now in risen glory and that in this trial there was being fulfilled for us Christ's prayer :

> Father,
> I want those you have given me
> to be with me where I am,
> so that they may always see the glory
> you have given me (*John* 17 : 24).

There is no greater human trial than a sense that one's life is a failure, one has let down one's friends, one is useless and of no value to anyone. Isaiah foretold that Christ would be such a failure, that he would be despised and we would take no account of him.

Christ's death seemed to the whole of his contemporaries, except perhaps only his mother, to be the defeat and disgrace of all he had ever promised, the collapse of all the hopes he had ever aroused, the discrediting of all he had ever said. Even the disciples ran away; it was no honour to be associated with him now. Even Peter reneged and swore that he didn't even know the man: it didn't pay to be thought to be one of his group now.

The conversation of the two disciples who were walking to Emmaus on the third day after his death revealed the sense of failure and the depths of depression that gripped the whole group. Their faces were downcast with the embarrassment of having to repeat to a stranger their topic of conversation. "Our own hope had been", they sadly confessed, "that he would be the one to set Israel free." (*Luke* 24 : 20.) But now it is all over, he is dead. All our hopes are buried in his grave.

But the moment of collapse of human hope is the moment of God's power. "Was it not ordained", the stranger said, "that the Christ should suffer and so enter into his glory." (*Luke* 24 :25.) The Cross which was an object of pious revulsion to the Jews, a weapon of invincible repression to the Romans and of paralysing fear to their victims, becomes through Christ an emblem of liberation, a sign of victory and glory. Because Christ endures its shame, the Cross now symbolises "Christ in us, our hope of glory".

THROUGH SUFFERING TO GLORY

But pain for Christ was not an end in itself. His suffering is no morbid, masochistic relishing of suffering for its own sake. He suffered for us, he suffered with us, in order to redeem suffering for us and make it, shared with him, a means of our sharing in his Resurrection. Through him, with him, in him, our suffering is transformed from despairing absurdity into confident hope of glory. When we suffer, we should always remember Christ's own words to the disciples on the Emmaus road : "Why look among the dead for someone who is alive?"

He is not here; he has risen (*Luke* 24 :5-6).

The last words of Jesus, like his first, are not about death but about life; not about the past, but about the future; not about the old but about the new. His last words are about the Spirit who is life : his last gesture is to give the Spirit.

Traditionally, we have known the last words of the Passion narrative in the form : "Bowing his head, he gave up the ghost", or "He gave up the Spirit". More correctly, these words mean :

Bowing his head (towards Mary and St John) he handed on the Spirit (*John* 19 :29-30).

The purpose and the consequence of his death is the handing on of his Spirit to the Church. Because of his death, we receive that Holy Spirit, the Spirit of life and power and victory, in our Mass today.

That Spirit is for us all the assurance that we can rise from our infirmities of body and of spirit, that our nation can rise from its tragedy and disgrace of today, can rise with Christ to a new future in his risen glory.

For this Spirit is the same Spirit as that of which we read in Ezekiel's prophecy. The prophet was asked by God to walk up and down through a valley strewn with blanched bones — a vivid symbol of the death and decay that is the final end of all merely human hopes. But, in the prophecy, the Spirit of God breathes upon these bones, and we read :

The breath entered them; they came to life again and stood up to their feet, a great, an immense throng.

The Lord explained the parable to the prophet in these words :

These bones are the whole House of Israel. They keep saying : "Our bones are dried up, our hope has gone; we are as good as dead." So say to them: "The Lord says this: I am now going to open your graves: I mean to raise you from your graves, my people, and lead you back to the soil of Israel . . . and I shall put my Spirit in you, and you will live" (*Ezekiel* 37 : 11-14).

The last word of the Passion is spoken by the Risen Lamb of God in the Book of the Apocalypse. On the occasion of news of personal tragedy, of dear ones medically sentenced, on the occasion of the death of those we love, in serious illness affecting ourselves or our loved ones, above the news bulletins and the pictures of daily tragedy and assassination, murder and disaster in our own country, let us listen for that Voice.

> Do not be afraid; it is I, the First and the Last; I am the living one. I was dead and now I am to live for ever and ever : and I hold the keys of death and of the under world (*Apocalypse* 1:17-18).

Part Four

The New Ireland

Completion of Ireland's struggle now can only be the patient effort of persuasion, the persevering labour of politics, the intelligent practice of democracy.

Forward from the Green Paper

An address to the Auditor's Paper at the Meeting of the College Theological Society, Trinity College, Dublin, on November 2nd, 1972.

I do not dissent from the Auditor's contention, namely that the situation in the North is a scandal for all Irish Christians in face of an onlooking increasingly de-Christianised world. There is no graver problem facing all the Irish Churches today.

SECTARIAN NOT RELIGIOUS

It is not a religious problem, but it is a sectarian one. The difference between these two is absolute. Few words are so misused nowadays as the word "sectarian". Sometimes it is made synonymous with "Catholic" or "Protestant" or "denominational". Thus, for example, Protestant or Catholic schools can be labelled "sectarian" and thus be subtly represented as divisive and reprehensible. A society composed of Catholics can be emotively smeared as a "Catholic sectarian State".

Sectarianism properly understood is hostility and suspicion directed against those who belong to a different religious denomination, or discriminatory practices in regard to them. In the Irish context, it is above all the assumption that one may or ought to discriminate socially, economically or politically between groups or individuals on religious-denominational lines. The OED has it that sectarianism is "undue favouring of a particular denomination". In all these cases, religious labels are clearly being used for non-religious purposes.

People, whether they intend it or not, are evincing sectarian tendencies if they betray awareness of people's religious affiliation in circumstances where religious affiliations as such are irrelevant — for example, when people are being given the franchise, or being electorally zoned, or admitted to or excluded from a political party; when they are applying for houses or seeking employment or tendering for contracts or being assessed in terms of "loyalty" or "security risk".

No-one can hold that education is irrelevant to religion; therefore "Protestant schools" are not a contradiction in terms. But "Protestant votes" or "Protestant jobs" should be seen as self-contradictory terms, just as much as "Catholic gunmen" or "Protestant terrorists". Catholics and Protestants should both protest, on religious grounds, against such abuses of language committed about either. These terms should be just as shocking as the absurdities we sometimes hear about "Catholic weapons", "Protestant barricades", or "Catholic or Protestant bombs and bullets".

FAILURE OF PARTITION

If sectarianism be the drawing of political distinctions between religious groups, then the partitioning of Ireland was a sectarian decision and its fruits could scarcely fail to be sectarian. This is meant to describe the 1922 decision, not to judge it. Some of the motives were honourable, deriving in part from a despairing conclusion that only a territorial division along roughly religious lines could bring any sort of peace to Ireland.

It is unhelpful to dwell morbidly and censoriously on that past decision. It is its subsequent results and continuing effects which should solely concern us. The conclusion is indisputable and it is now, for the first time in fifty years, admitted by most observers that this decision was a mistake and that the political institutions derived from it in the area thus partitioned have significantly failed. This is the unmistakable conclusion of the British Government's Green Paper on *The Future of Northern Ireland,* which has just been published[7].

THE GREEN PAPER

The Green Paper makes an historic re-appraisal of British Government thinking about Ireland. The Paper penetratingly diagnoses the inherent defect of the Northern Ireland political institutions of fifty years.

This defect is traced by the Paper to the adoption of United Kingdom conventions regarding parliamentary democracy, and in particular that of majority rule, in a territory where these conventions had consequences entirely different from those entailed in the neighbouring island. Specifically these conventions were adopted without account being taken of the "special feature of the Northern Ireland situation, (namely) that the great divide in political life was not between different viewpoints . . . but between two whole communities". *(Op. cit. 14, p. 5).* This led to the creation of a "permanent majority" unlikely to cultivate sensitivity, and a "permanent minority" unlikely to develop responsibility. In this situation, discrimination and injustice were almost inevitable. Complaints of them and protests about them were, the Green Paper admits, sometimes "undoubtedly justified". Suspicions of them were, in any case, inevitable. "What is incontestable", the document states, "is that the continuous and complete control of central government by representatives of the majority alone was virtually bound to give rise to such suspicions". *(Op. cit. 14, p. 5.)*

Many in Ireland, in a first hasty and sometimes safe-playing reaction to the Green Paper, do not seem to me to have revealed awareness of how radical a revision of historic British attitudes it represents, how honest and earnest an attempt it constitutes to reach an objective and impartial analysis. Extremist unionists are shown more and more as determined to be "British" in a sense which Her Majesty Queen Elizabeth's government and the public they represent no longer are. Extremist republicans are exposed as doctrinaire haters of a Britain which in large measure and in obvious will and desire no longer exists.

"TALK OF IRISH UNITY"

The Green Paper is unprecedented in the history of Westminster — Northern Ireland relationships also in officially recognising the "Irish dimension" of the Northern Ireland problem. Its reiteration of successive Westminster pledges regarding the "Constitutional position" is expressly stated not to "preclude the necessary taking into account of . . . the Irish Dimension". The "present status" of Northern Ireland is significantly juxtaposed with a reference to "the possibility — which would have to be compatible with the principle of consent — of subsequent change in the status". *(Op. cit. 76-8, pp. 33-4)*

The extraordinary paradox about some recent claims that talk of Irish unity is positively harmful is that their authors do not seem to have realised that they were in fact asking of Irish nationalists a degree of dumbness which the British Government is not asking of them. Even unionist leaders have had to admit that advocating and working by non-violent means towards the reunification of Ireland is a legitimate political aim and have urged unionists to begin to learn to co-exist with parties and movements committed to a United Ireland and therefore explicitly not conforming to traditional unionist test of "loyalty".

This is the least that political realism and plain honesty and truth require. We can apply here words used by the Green Paper in the context of the division of powers and responsibilities between Westminster and Northern Ireland, and say that silence about Irish unity is a "prescription for confusion and misunderstanding", by introducing "ambiguity in the relationship " between the two communities in Northern Ireland. (*Op. cit. 79(c), p. 35.*)

There can be no hope of any peaceful co-existence until each community recognises the right to exist of the other community, precisely as the other community understands itself and affirms its own traditions and loyalties. Nationalists and republicans simply must stop pretending that unionists are lapsed United Irishmen, merely requiring a push from Britain or a pamphlet from republican headquarters to bring them back into the Tone tradition. Unionists must simply stop claiming that nationalists are secret unionists, prevented by republican intimidation or Catholic educational indoctrination from avowing their attachment to the British connection.

Talk about Irish unity is not merely permissible, it is essential if any sort of normality is to return to Northern Ireland. The Green Paper implicitly recognises this when it speaks of new institutions whose primary purpose must be "to seek a much wider consensus than has hitherto existed". When a minority is explicitly committed to a United Ireland, then talk about Irish unity is an obvious condition of the Green Paper's aim of "assuring minority groups of an effective voice and a real influence", and even more of "giving minority interests a share in the exercise of executive power". (*Op. cit. 79(d), p. 35.*)

The Green Paper goes further in indicating the requirements of a truly democratic system in Northern Ireland :

> On the other hand, it can be argued that the British democratic system only works where a regular alternation of parties is possible; that the real test of a democratic system is its ability to provide peaceful and orderly government, and that other countries with divided communities have made special constitutional provision to ensure participation by all; that a number of these countries have had stable and successful coalition governments over many years and that there is no hope of binding the minority to the support of new political arrangements in Northern Ireland unless they are admitted to active participation in any new structures. (*Op. cit. 58, pp. 62-7.*)

Elsewhere we read :

> A Northern Ireland assembly or authority must be capable of involving all its members constructively in ways which satisfy them and those they represent that the whole community has a part to play in the government of the Province. As a minimum this would involve assuring minority groups of an effective voice and a real influence; but there are strong arguments that the objective of real participation should be achieved by giving minority interests a share in the exercise of executive power if this can be achieved by means which are not unduly complex or artificial, and which do not represent an obstacle to effective government. (*Op. cit. 79(f), pp. 26-36.*)

POLITICAL REFORMS

One of the new positive contributions of the Green Paper is its indication of the commitment of the British

Government to radical reform of the political structures of Northern Ireland, with the over-riding object of building into the new structures an assurance "that there will be absolute fairness and equality of opportunity for all". (*Op. cit. 79(h), p. 36.*) The Green Paper declares, of course, that reform of structures will not do more than present "an opportunity for progress". Progress can then ensue only from a change "in the hearts and minds of the people of Northern Ireland". (*Op. cit. 83, p. 37.*)

This statement of priorities seems to me to be absolutely right and in fact to be a more Christian assessment of the relations of political action to moral and spiritual reform than that sometimes suggested by churchmen. Some statements of Christians to the effect that what we need first and perhaps only is reconciliation, love, brotherhood, could, I fear, very understandably be stigmatised by the old Marxist catch-cry of "pie in the sky". I can understand John Elsom's bitter remark: "The man who says that all human problems could be solved by love is bluntly a fool."

The Christian moral and spiritual command to love one another includes the political imperative to create structures which make love possible and meaningful and to reform the structures and institutions and conventions which make love difficult or leave it without its condition and content, which is justice, and political, social and economic equality.

Denunciations of sectarianism will be ineffectual so long as the institutions continue to reflect and to perpetuate sectarianism. Denunciations of violence will be ineffectual so long as the political structures continue to create a frustrated minority perpetually deprived of political power and of participation in the making of the decisions which affect their destiny.

The first step to be taken is not reconciliation but reform, and most immediately political reform. The first duty of churchmen now is to proclaim this priority. Reconciliation is always and immutably what Christians *ought* to do and preach; it must be also made what we churchmen *can* do ourselves and lead our people to do, without insult to their human dignity or injury to their human rights. It is in this direction that the Green Paper points.

THE PLEBISCITE

The Plebiscite, whose terms have just been announced, unfortunately does not measure up to the best standards of the Green Paper. The plebiscite, in the simplistic form in which its questions are framed, can only be divisive, backward-looking, sterile. It will merely, one more weary time, divide people along the predictable lines. Nothing new will be discovered or created.

We have had plebiscite after plebiscite through fifty embittered years of community division. We have, in effect, never had any political consultations of the electorate except plebiscites. All Northern Ireland elections were virtually turned by the politicians into plebiscites on the constitutional issue. These plebiscite-elections presupposed a division into a dominant and a defeated community and they further consolidated this division. Replay of this out-of-date recording can bring no joy to those who long for a new Ulster and a new Ireland.

Delay and indecisiveness only give the men of violence in the two communities time to continue their evil work of dividing, intimidating, terrorising and demolishing, for more and more people, the last vestiges of civilised living.

SECTARIAN CIVIL WAR

I believe that the fear of sectarian civil war should not
be allowed by the authorities to deter them from these
reforms. It is not that this awful danger is unreal. It is
rather that the sectarian civil war situation already
exists. How many deaths, how many sectarian assassinations, how much sectarian intimidation and expulsion
of families from their homes and schools and neighbourhoods, how many profanations and destructions of
churches have to occur before we call it sectarian civil
war?

We must not allow fear of the worst that could happen
to make us complacent or fatalistic about the evil and the
horror of what is happening daily now. The doom that
threatens Northern Ireland is not so much a Doomsday
blood-bath, but just a slow, unending continuation of
the daily passions, hatreds and cruelties which are
breaking hearts and lives, corrupting consciences and
destroying Christianity.

It is so easy for us in the lounges of the Republic to be
complacent or even smugly superior about the sufferings
of the little people of both communities in the North.
One of the great obstacles to reconciliation and eventual
reunification in Ireland is that, not only do the two
Northern communities not "identify" with one another,
but that so many of us in the Republic do not really
"identify" with either. We so easily dismiss them both
as bigots; their problems are of their own making, we
think; we feel better off without them; we are almost
secretly glad that Britain has to cope with them, not
we. More and more, both communities in the North are
coming to feel not understood and not wanted either
by Britain or by the Republic, as the case may be.

For many in the Republic, the Protestant and the

unionist community are aliens, Cromwellian colonists, "other", not "our people in the North". For many others, irrespective of religious affiliation, the Catholics in the North are religiously retarded, socially inferior, and politically unenlightened. They are a political irrelevance. They are not "interesting".

Jacques Ellul, in his book on *Violence,* makes the point that Christian concern about the poor is sometimes selective. Christians unconsciously distinguish between the "interesting poor" and the "uninteresting poor". He says :

> The interesting poor are those whose defence is in reality an attack against Europe, against capitalism, against the U.S.A. The uninteresting poor represent forces that are considered passé. Their struggle concerns themselves only. They are fighting not to destroy a capitalist or colonialist regime, but simply to survive as individuals, as a culture, a people. And that, of course, is not at all interesting, is it?

Ellul's point is painful. I think its hurt is medicinal. It is undeniably fashionable in some quarters in the Republic to regard Northern Catholics or Northern Protestants, as the case may be, as "uninteresting poor".

SEGREGATED SCHOOLS

What of the Churches? What can or should they do? The Auditor suggests "desegregating the schools" and thinks it is "likely that this would result in instilling the spirit of brotherhood in the young people of tomorrow". The suggestion is very often made and it seems attractive. I must say that I regard it as belonging in the same category as is seen as "reconciliation before political change". Without drastic change in community attitudes, and therefore in the political structures which perpetuate those attitudes, to talk of "desegregated schooling" is to play with ideas and words.

With every week that passes, Belfast and Derry are being divided, more implacably than ever they were before, into Protestant and Catholic "reservations", outside of which no adult, much less any child, feels safe. If Catholic children are being molested on their way to their own Catholic schools, or prevented from attending them, and their families being forced out of their own school neighbourhoods, it is glaringly unrealistic to speak of Catholic children being welcomed into county schools side by side with Protestant children. It is precisely in the areas which lack the spirit of brotherhood that united schooling is hopelessly impracticable.

Professor Richard Rose studied the question of separate schools in his book *Governing Without Consensus*. He would personally favour religiously mixed schools, as do many people at a distance from the actual community situation. But he admits that his research lends little support to his personal views. I quote :

> Non-denominational education in Northern Ireland, like desegregation of schools in America, is often valued because mixed schools are expected to encourage friendliness between groups. Proponents also expect non-denominational schooling to reduce political discord. There are sufficient persons with a mixed education to measure how such exposure affects political outlooks. The surprising conclusion is that, while attendance at mixed schools tends to reduce ultra and rebel views, it does so only to a very limited extent. . . . The limited effect of separate education is consistent with a variety of studies elsewhere of Catholic and state schools.

The failure of mixed schooling to have more influence upon political outlooks may be explained in at least two ways. Education is but one among a multitude of formal and informal influences upon political attitudes. Inasmuch as a child's school is effectively determined by his parents' ascribed religion, then schooling can do little about differences that exist before a child commences education. Another possible explanation is that a better understanding of the opposite religion gained by integrated education will not necessarily lead to greater trust. A Catholic in a mixed school may learn that when Protestants say "Not an inch" they mean it, just as a Protestant may learn that his Catholic classmates refuse to regard the Union Jack as the flag to which they give allegiance. The limited extent to which mixed education affects attitudes is not sufficient to justify its introduction on the ground that political discord can be ended by integrating schools. This would require years of negotiation about existing institutions and to establish new schools. Then, it would literally take generations before the bulk of the adult population of Northern Ireland had been exposed to the weak ameliorating influence of mixed education.

But the crisis in Northern Ireland is now. Any "solution" which would take generations to produce a "weak ameliorating influence" is not a solution.

But there are more fundamental considerations. To suggest that separate schools foster community bitterness would be a slur on one of the most dedicated, committed and responsible bodies of people in both communities, the teachers. Do we realise the struggle these men and women have, day after day, week after week, to teach Christian love to people who experience it almost only in school; to educate away from violence children whose entire non-school time is pervaded by violence, violence from republican guerillas or UDA commandos, from shoot-and-accelerate sectarian killers, or from security forces?

Separate schools are the only escape from hate and violence and fear the children have. The teachers are, with the clergy, the best influence for peace the children know. Let us salute and admire them, not impute to them the blame of others, including politicians.

What would, however, be helpful in improving community relations in the long term — though probably this too must, in the areas of greatest community tension, await a more propitious moment — would be more involvement of Catholic and Protestant children, at all school levels, in common out-of-school activities, like playgrounds, athletics, outings, field trips, projects, debates, etc.

The basic Christian formation of the school would thus find opportunity to translate itself into tolerant, enlightened and truly Christian personal relations in the life situation for which school prepares. The two religious and cultural and historic traditions could thus mutually stimulate and enrich each other, without either having to be submerged in a colourless and mean little secular orthodoxy.

THE CHURCHES' RESPONSIBILITY

The Auditor sounds a note of urgency and indeed crisis for the Churches. He is perfectly right. It is a crisis of and for Christianity. Crisis means judgement. Christians, leaders and laity, are being judged, and not only by men but also by God, in this situation. The Judgement is for each of us. Let us not, to indulge our feelings of moral superiority, make scapegoats of others.

Above all, let us not lightly judge our brothers in the North. No-one has the right to read *ad clerums* to the clergy in the North who does not remember that two of them, Father Hugh Mullen and Father Noel Fitzpatrick,

died of gunshot wounds, martyrs of Christian reconciliation; and spent their last conscious moments leading the
bystanders in a prayer that repeated the Master's prayer :
"Father, forgive them, they do not know what they are
doing."

No-one can preach reconciliation who has not humbled
himself at the thought of Rev. Joseph Parker, who went
on television to speak and ask forgiveness for his son's
killers, and who fasted in the night and the cold to
preach forgiveness to those whose ears were deaf to
words.

No-one has the right to speak of prophecy who has not
reflected on what it takes to go, by day and by night,
through gunfire to bring the sacraments and the comforting of Christ to the wounded or the injured.

Let us humbly recognise our unworthiness to give
advice or exhortation to the priests and clergy of all
denominations who preach reconciliation amid the
bombs and the bullets and the volleys of stones. The
Auditor will, I hope, pardon me if I refer to his phrase
about "a weekly statement abhorring violence and urging
restraint". The latter seems suddenly less banal and
more significant when one tries to put oneself in the
place of those clergy who weekly deplore violence and
urge restraint in the pulpits of Falls Road, Ardoyne and
Willowfield, Sandy Row, The Shankill and Bally-
macarret.

CHRISTIAN PROPHECY

But it is prophetic utterance which the North needs of
churchmen at the present time. Thomas Merton, hours
before his untimely death, said : "The problem for
monasticism is not survival but prophecy[8]".

We can apply his words to Christian churchmen today.

What all we churchmen need to aspire to today is not survival but prophecy. Prophets have never been noted for referring back to assemblies or consulting the flocks. We must all get away, not so much from the syndrome of the "priest-ridden people", but from that of the lay-ridden clergy. For far too long many clergy have been almost in the position that is caricatured in the question: "Where is that crowd going? — for I am its leader. Where is that parade going? — for I am its chaplain."

Sectarianism is political exploitation of religious ignorance. But religious ignorance itself is a pastoral problem. It must be tackled vigorously, by something like Christian missionary effort, but here at home, and not only in the not yet Christian lands overseas. It must be met, not by less Christian education, but by more, and more explicitly Christian education and formation. The sickness of the North is not too much Christianity but too little. The trouble is not with Christianity but with distortions and degenerations of Christianity which answer to the term sectarianism.

POLITICIANS' RESPONSIBILITY

But the prophetic voice must not cease to proclaim that the paramount responsibility rests with the politicians to introduce reforms. They must not cease to preach the Christian obligation of their followers to accept them. It is the three Governments concerned and all the political parties who must assume their responsibilities. The Green Paper provides a real basis for hope of a new future for all communities and peoples in Ireland and indeed in these British and Irish islands.

May politicians show now the courage and magnanimity which President de Valera, then Taoiseach, showed in an historic broadcast in 1945, when Anglo-Irish relations were as strained and feeling as high as

they are now. It was 17th May, 1945; he was replying
to a broadcast by Mr Winston Churchill. He said :

> I sincerely trust that it is not (by violence) that our
> ultimate unity and freedom will be achieved. . . . In
> latter years, I have had a vision of a nobler and
> better ending, better for both our people and for
> the future of mankind. For that I have now been
> long working. . . . As a community which has been
> mercifully spared from all the major sufferings as
> well as from the blinding hates and rancours en-
> gendered by the recent war, we shall endeavour to
> render thanks to God by playing a Christian part in
> helping, so far as a small nation can, to bind up some
> of the gaping wounds of suffering humanity.

The wounds are now nearer home. They are in our own
body.

The Challenge
of the New Ireland

An article first published in The Cross, *November 7th,
1972. It is reprinted by permission of the Editor.*

There has been much talk about a New Ireland, but
there is a danger that this could become a new escapist
slogan, another cliche among many in our recent
history. The trouble about slogans is that they become
a lazy substitute for both thought and action. They
flatter us with the pleasing illusion of having solved a
problem, whereas we have only bewitched ourselves
with our own fine talk. We will not just talk a New
Ireland into reality. In the particular context of finding
a solution to the Northern crisis and working towards
the eventual unity of Ireland, honesty and realism are
among the first things necessary.

We have talked for years about the "re-integration of
the national territory" and have indeed given this
phrase an honoured place in the Constitution of Ireland.
Many similar phrases, like those of "asserting the right
of the Irish Parliament and Government to exercise
jurisdiction over the whole island of Ireland", "liberating occupied Ireland", "completing the struggle for
independence", although they were understandable in
the wake of a War of Independence which was only
partially successful, need to be reflected on more deeply
now, fifty years later.

IMPOSSIBLE TO OBLITERATE

This is necessary, first of all because it is impossible now simply to obliterate fifty years of history. The very existence of partition, the operation throughout half a century of two separate States, with the totally diverse development of educational structures, social and medical services, different mass media, all have created deep-seated and complex divergences of experience, outlook and cultural pattern. Partition, of course, has not simply created the differences; it resulted from existing differences and in turn consolidated those differences. Partition gave government embodiment to that composite of convictions, loyalties, values, emotions, prejudices and fears, which is Northern unionism.

Stating the fundamental injustice and error of the 1922 "solution" of the Irish question is one thing — and much evidence has accumulated in fifty years to corroborate the truth of the remark attributed to none other than Sir Edward Carson, that few more harmful things could happen to Ireland than its division along religious lines. But to face up honestly and realistically to the situation left us by fifty years of separate Irish Parliaments and Governments is another thing entirely. To seek to go forward from the situation of 1972 to rebuild a lost unity in circumstances far removed from those of 1922 is still another.

The second reason why reappraisal of some of our cherished slogans and ingrained attitudes is now necessary is that they tend to mis-state the problem and to lead us away from the path to solutions.

Most of our traditional republican formulae simply ignore the existence of the Northern unionist fact. But there is no magic whereby this massive fact can be made just go away. There are nearly a million unionists in the North who simply do not share or even under-stand the republican attitudes and principles which we take for granted. They do not feel unfree, or British-occupied. There is no physical way in which they could be coerced by anyone into building one nation with us on our traditional terms.

The phrases I have mentioned above are mis-placed in particular because they suggest the mere absorption of the unionist population into our existing State, or the extension to the whole island of the authority exercised at present by the Dublin Parliament and Government over 26 counties.

CONSENT NOT CONQUEST

These notions have in common a certain suggestion of domination or conquest, which merely arouses belliger-ency on the unionist side. What seems from a repub-lican point of view liberation of the North, seems from the unionist perspective aggression from the South. What we see as re-integration of the national territory appears in unionist eyes as a threat of occupation of their territory by a government other than their own. What we see as the self-evident right of Ireland to unity, unionists read as unjust usurpation.

To point out these unpalatable facts is not popular. It is easier to let republican sentiment or passion or mere habit over-simplify the issues. A modern writer on violence has said that "Violence expresses the habit of simplification of situations, political, social or human." Because our republican tradition has been, however justifiably, a violent one it inclines us now to a danger-ous and over-simplified view of the Northern problem. We must be prepared to make the sacrifice of our own deepest sentiment, and to run the risk of misunderstanding and unpopularity, if we are to evolve a renewed republican philosophy applicable to a re-united Ireland.

This new philosophy will have to be non-violent. It will also have to be social — directing against social abuses and deficiencies at home the aggressive energies that formerly needed to be directed against a foreign foe. We would not thus be betraying our own most basic and national and even republican tradition. The struggle for religious emancipation, for the franchise, for ownership of the land, were social revolutions which laid the foundation for democracy and for ultimate independence. They were essentially non-violent. They stand still as proof of the effectiveness of skilfully organised and led non-violent action.

SOCIAL REVOLUTION

Side by side with the violent struggle for political independence went the commitment to non-violent social revolution as the end and fruit of the violent struggle. The goals of this non-violent social revolution, to be pursued when political freedom was won, were spelled out in the Democratic Programme of the First Dáil. Much of it is still very far from realisation. The relevant republican philosophy for today could begin with re-stating that Programme as national policy. This would be both fidelity to the old republican Ireland and commitment to the building of the New Ireland.

Such a philosophy would also be intelligible to, and capable of being shared with, the unionists of the North. Their particular form of the Protestant political tradition had, after all, a significant contribution to make to American democracy. The Protestant tradition which they share helped to shape British democracy and the democratic and non-ideological version of Socialism which is distinctively British.

Some claim that the Northern Presbyterian alignment with Wolfe Tone was a fortuitous and temporary phenomenon, uncharacteristic and unlikely to recur. This is probably a somewhat superficial view. Political radicalism and non-conformity is a deep-seated tradition of Presbyterianism. Social involvement is a cherished tradition with Protestantism generally. Social Christianity and social reform or social revolution are concepts Protestants will share with us.

In making our own part of Ireland more just, we can also be making union with us less unthinkable and eventually more attractive for Northern unionists, not merely economically — for man does not live by economic criteria alone — but also morally and spiritually.

The Northern crisis should be seen by all of us in the Republic as a moral challenge, an urgent invitation to make our own society more progressive, more just, more democratic. We need strong motivation to arouse us from a certain political torpor, a degree of smugness in our new-found economic well-being, an undeniable apathy or defeatism about social evils, a persisting resistance to social change and social reform. Our readiness for reform in our own society will be a good measure of our sincerity in seeking reunion with the North.

A PLURALIST SOCIETY
The New Ireland we hope to create for the 32 counties will have to be a pluralist society. It could not be too often stated that a pluralist society is quite distinct from a secular society. A Christian society can be and should

be pluralist. A secular society cannot be, as such, a Christian society. What we should be seeking now as the blue-print of a new society are the Christian principles common to all our Christian traditions on which we can agree, rather than some colourless de-Christianised, aseptic formula which will offend no-one because it will leave all completely uninspired, unchallenged and uninterested.

Our search for constitutional blue-prints should not be limited to carbon copies from the desks of our nearest neighbours. Not a few of our "futurologists", who so learnedly and so confidently predict the pattern of our future in Ireland, turn out to be merely stating a version of what Britain or America are doing now, and declaring that that is what we shall be or ought to be doing in the future. A valid answer can sometimes take the form of a recent writer's comment on contemporary California : "I have seen the future; and it doesn't work." We can frequently say to the futurologists : "This is a possible future, if we want it; but it needn't happen unless we want it." Better still, we can go on to say : "It won't happen, because we don't want it."

LARGE IN MIND AND SPIRIT
There is no reason why we cannot shape an Irish Ireland large enough in mind and spirit to encompass all its diverse religious, cultural and political traditions in creative tension, rather than mutually destructive discord; an Ireland deeply Christian with a Christianity which remembers always that the greatest of all Christian things is love.

Will the New Generation build a better Ireland?

*An address to the National Federation of Youth Clubs'
Conference, held in the Franciscan College, Gormans-
town, on January 6th, 1973.*

We are much concerned nowadays about "the youth
problem" in our society and are perhaps sometimes
prone to feel that it is unprecedented and threatens the
whole future of society. But it is necessary to keep a
sense of historical proportion and perspective. Few
things help so much to keep our balance in the present
as an objective knowledge of our past.

In the present connection, it is salutary to remember that
this is not the first age to complain of a youth problem
and that the middle-aged men of today are not the first
to have lamented and denounced the deviant views and
behaviour of the young. Five hundred years before
Christ, a contemporary of Socrates spoke of youth in
these disparaging terms :

> Children today love luxury. They have bad manners,
> contempt for authority, a disrespect for their elders,
> and they talk instead of work. They contradict their
> parents, chatter before company, gobble up the best
> of the table and tyrannise their teachers.

This has quite a contemporary ring. There has always
been a generation gap, always a youth problem. The
middle-aged and older have always criticised and

slightly feared the young. Today's youth problem may differ in degree of intensity and in the extent of its repercussions. It is not an essentially new problem for humanity.

Those no longer young feel themselves challenged, threatened by the young. The feeling is sometimes provoked by arrogant and aggressive behaviour on the part of young people. But even when this is not so, the challenge and the threat are inherent in the situation and in the relationships between the generations. Every generation seems to need a scapegoat as a way of escaping from its own awareness of responsibility. For the not-so-young, a convenient scapegoat is youth. For young people themselves, a serviceable scapegoat can be their parents' generation, their parents' whole society, society itself and its institutions.

NEEDED REFORMS

That society and its institutions certainly need reforms; therefore the impatience of youth is understandable and admirable. That society and its institutions have undeniable merits, placing them before any others Ireland has known in centuries. They have enabled a degree of wellbeing to be achieved by great numbers of the Irish people such as Ireland has never experienced before, and of which the youth of today are privileged beneficiaries. Therefore the reaction of older people to extreme manifestations of youthful protest and impatience are understandable and justified. It is vitally important that each side of the generation gap make real efforts to see the other dispassionately and to know itself objectively.

The earlier generation seems to the young to be conservative, cautious, and afraid of change, of venture and of risk, committed to the status quo. There is much truth in the charge but not everything in the attitudes thus criticised is reprehensible. The older generation is after all the only generation of Irishmen ever to have effected a successful revolution, leading to the establishment of genuinely free and native institutions. Is it surprising that they should value those institutions, seek to conserve them, resent intemperate criticisms of them, be suspicious of those who seem more concerned to destroy those institutions than convinced and convincing about what they would then put in their place?

THE UNFINISHED REVOLUTION

The older generation were right to guard and conserve their revolution. But they had not sufficiently reflected on what conserving a revolution means. For the Irish revolution should have been seen, not so much as revolution won but as revolution begun.

What was accomplished by the struggle of 1916 to 1922 was freedom to work for freedom, independence to achieve social justice. It had in fact been true that the connection with England had been the source of most of our national and social evils. But it by no means followed that once the connection had been broken, these ills had *ipso facto* been cured. Indeed the late Father John Hayes used to say that all we had done was to break the least important of all the connections with England, the political one, leaving our subservience to England in the economic and cultural spheres as strong as ever.

Of course, the political connection had a unique importance. Until it had been broken, we had not the indispensable right to control our own destinies, and therefore lacked the power to strike off the other chains that bound us. But the mistake of the generation which fought for freedom was that it tended to think of political independence as an end in itself, rather than as a means to an end.

The founding generation of the Irish State lived in the euphoric memory of the Easter Proclamation and the Declaration of Independence. They had, for the most part, thought little enough about what independence was for or what sort of Ireland was to follow its establishment.

Military revolutions have limited objectives. They simplify complex issues. It seems to be of the essence of revolutionary violence that it simplifies issues. The danger of violent revolution is that when successful it refuses to de-simplify. Simplification always involves mystification.

National and social realities and ills are complex. When single, simple causes and culprits are accused, this is frequently a search for a scapegoat. When single and simple remedies are proned, this usually is a piece of political mystification. Both of these are phenomena of escapism, evasion of responsibility. The successful makers of the Irish revolution were only acting like most successful revolutionaries in resenting any de-simplification of their achievement. Yet this de-simplification was only part of a necessary de-mystification of their political revolution.

The de-simplification and de-mystification were already in fact inherent in the "canonical writings" of the Irish revolution. The Democratic Programme was a noble, if still embryonic and somewhat more rhetorical than researched and realistic attempt to sketch a post-revolutionary programme which the armed revolution would not accomplish but merely make possible. But this in itself amounted to a substantial de-simplification of the Easter Proclamation.

But for fifty years the Democratic Programme remained
a largely unread and unremembered text. Two generations of free Irishmen had been nurtured on the stirring
and noble rhetoric of the Easter Proclamation. About
what was to follow this, we were vague. About what did
in fact follow this, we were defensive, sensitive and
hence aggressive.

The Democratic Programme was essentially peripheral
to our romantic-mythical national view of 1916. So
dominant and unchallengeable was this view as late as
1966 that, when it was decided to honour the revolution
permanently in all the nation's schools, everyone
assumed this meant having a framed copy of the Easter
Proclamation in a place of honour in every school-
house; and no one thought of placing beside it the
equally "canonical" and even more relevant text of the
Democratic Programme.

MYTH OF VIOLENCE

The most serious defect of the first generation of Irish
freedom was the romantic glorification of revolutionary
violence which so strongly marked its popular version
of history. The battles were told over and over again in
increasingly epic language and glowing glorificatory
rhetoric, in multiplied national commemorative rituals,
in popular story-telling and personal reminiscence. The
battles were fought over and over again in parliamentary exchanges and in election speeches. Our political
thinking remained trapped for years in the categories of
the struggle for independence and our political align-
ments were determined for decades and indeed are
largely determined still by the options taken in its
immediate aftermath.

Simplification of issues, identification of and moral
detestation of enemies, seem to be necessary ingredients

in a successful revolution. But they remained characteristics of our post-revolutionary politics for most of fifty years in Ireland.

Irish revolutionaries were in all this no different from revolutionaries everywhere and at all times. The revolutionary after all has staked his all on the rightness and value of his revolution. It has been the most powerful presence in his life, the most determinative influence on his personality, the most dramatic experience of his life-time. The temptation to live emotionally in the remembered, recalled and re-dramatised revolutionary past rather than see it as prelude to an undramatic, unglamorous, politically reformist present, is too strong for most revolutionaries.

The leaders of the successful revolution are normally the first politicians of the post-revolutionary period. They virtually write the popular history of the revolution, create the official mythology of the revolution. The whole national self-understanding becomes inevitably deeply coloured by their emotional involvement with and euphoric experience of revolution. Any attempt at historical detachment is easily represented as unpatriotic. The search for scholarly objectivity is quickly classed with the anti-national propaganda of the ancient enemy. Simplification of issues and identification of hate-objects is in any case emotionally satisfying, and de-simplication tends to be resented as betrayal.

The Irish revolutionaries were in fact incomparably less violent, less vengeful, less propagandist and less repressive, than most revolutionaries in this or other centuries have been. And yet the cost of the revolutionary mythology in this country has been very high.

Our whole concept of patriotism had been distorted

and deformed. Love of country has been misshapen into hatred of its enemies, foreign and native. Ireland has been loved emotionally, romantically, loved as an idealised abstraction, rather than as people, people with needs creating responsibilities in us, with rights to hold their differences. Love of Ireland has been identified with fighting for Ireland rather than working for Ireland, in other words with killing and destroying, rather than serving living Irishmen, so that a better style of living in Ireland may be enjoyed by all the children of the nation equally. When we sang together, it was patriotic songs; but patriotic songs meant songs of gun and blood, not songs of people to be loved, helped, served. And in each decade since independence, many young men of twenty have gone out again to kill and to die, because they loved Ireland but knew no other way of loving her, had been taught and shown no other way, but the way of the patriotic songs.

NORTHERN PROBLEM

Nowhere has the identification of patriotism with violent revolution, the simplification of national problems and romantic-mystical reading of Irish history been more harmful than in the area of our attitudes towards the Northern problem. The social revolution in Ireland was retarded and even our awareness of social problems impeded by our view of the revolution as military struggle and as having happened and needing only to be celebrated. In a similar way we were rendered incapable of objective and informed thinking about the Northern problem by the stereotyped, simplified version of it which became national orthodoxy and popular sentiment. Indeed we did not feel a need to think about the Northern problem at all, since both the explanation of the problem and its eventual solution were given without thought but with great emotional satisfaction in terms of the national myth.

So the nation was left content to believe that we would be morally justified in principle in using physical force to liberate the North, though in practice we did not have the force and in fact would not use it, or at least not now and in fact probably never.

But young men were more impatient, perhaps more consistent and even possibly more honest, when they trained and drilled and bought guns and inevitably then used them. The young took the songs literally when the older ones were only indulging sentiment. The Six Counties remained for both the only remaining foreign-occupied corner of Ireland, the fourth green field not yet cleared of the invader and the stranger, the not yet liberated *irredenta*, left as business still to be completed from the unfinished struggle for full national independence.

This national and quasi-official version of the Northern problem shared with national mystification or myth-ology the characteristics that it is completely rounded off, all-explanatory, emotionally satisfying, nationally gratifying and a perfect substitute for any further thinking and indeed any kind of action about the problem. Contrary facts were irritants, interrupting the flow of the rhetoric and such as would be dragged into the debate only by people of dubious national record.

But such contrary facts included the devastating reality that nearly a million people in that fourth green field did not feel themselves invaders or strangers at all, did not feel unfree or in need of liberation at all, did not feel occupied by foreign troops but rather in danger of occupation by their neighbours and would-be liberators.

In other words, nearly a million people live in Ireland,

where they have lived in their own homes and lands and industries for more than three hundred years; but they do not share our view of Irish history, do not accept our concept of nationhood, do not experience our patriotic emotions, do not share our national aims. You cannot coerce nearly a million people — and the reason is not that one has not sufficient physical force to do so, but that it is morally wrong to do so, even if one had the physical power to do it successfully.

In many respects, the national myth which was an almost necessary ingredient in our successful revolution and an almost inevitable consequence of that revolution's success, has been a fatal hindrance to any realistic analysis of the Northern problem; but a realistic analysis is an indispensable condition of any search for a solution.

THE ULSTER COUNTER-MYTH

The same of course would have to be said about the exactly parallel counter-myth created by the armed revolt which established Northern Ireland as a state. "Ulster" too developed its mythology, its romantic-mystical politico-religious myth, carefully fostered by the politicians, regarded too complacently by other community leaders.

The Ulster myth too would tolerate no statement of, allow no recognition of, disagreeable contrary fact. It ignored the existence within its own State and territory of nearly half a million people, more than a third of its population, whose home had always been Ulster, but an Ulster totally differently understood, totally otherwise loved. Here were Ulstermen who did not share the official version of history, did not feel conscious of any sort of emotional identification with the State, of any moral duty of allegiance to it. Their existence could not be ignored. Their right to exist and to hold, assert and work peacefully for their dissenting political views should never have been questioned, could not effectively be repressed and can now never again be denied.

DEMYTHOLOGISING

The demythologising of the Republic's history has been painful, and is still far from complete; but it is in progress and all responsible leaders and groups are now wholeheartedly committed to it. The demythologising of Ulster's history has, at popular level at any rate, not even been begun. Influential politicians are actively obstructing it. Too many other community leaders still do not even seem to see the need for it. There is no time left.

There is no future for Ulster or for Ireland until we all in this island accept with equal calmness and conviction two related axioms : you cannot coerce nearly a million Protestants into a united Ireland; you cannot coerce nearly half a million Catholics into a united, in the sense of unionist, Ulster.

VIOLENCE AND COUNTER-VIOLENCE

Ireland is not the only country with a problem of violence, even of politically or socially motivated violence. In Ireland, political violence has a particular historical origin and assumes distinctive emotional and cultural expression. But violence in one form or another is a problem facing all modern society. No society can nowadays hope to survive unless it can find valid, just and effective ways of coping with the threat of the violence of revolution or at least the violence of protest.

Experience in the past four years in Ireland, like experience elsewhere, shows that once organised violence is unleashed, it becomes almost impossible to control. The classical methods of military repression and counter-violence which governments invoke to defeat it may be effective in the short term, but they have failure built into their very success. The methods they use morally corrupt the society which uses them, discredit the authority which sanctions them, ensure a perpetuation of resentment and a future propensity to renewed violence in those sectors of the population where violence has been for the moment violently suppressed.

Meanwhile, violence and repression mutually feed one another and conspire to produce a new and evil anti-morality of violence, where the end is held to justify the means, the results are counted sufficient exculpation of the vilest methods on one side or the other, and sincerity of purpose or goodness of intended result are believed to make the foulest methods right. A generation of children and adolescents is habituated to hold human life cheap and treat the most sacred human rights and values with brutal cynicism.

FROM REVOLUTION TO REFORM

The conclusion one seems obliged to draw is that the only way a society can cope with violence is to try to anticipate its outbreak and prevent resort to it. For this, it is necessary to remedy in time the conditions, the injustices and grievances which prompt men to violent protest. It is therefore necessary for the modern state to have antennae sensitive to social problems and to all forms of human need. It is necessary for modern government to have a well thought out and dynamic social philosophy, realistically orientated towards policies and practices of social justice. Putting it more simply and more effectively, it is the first duty of statesmen today to have a well-informed and committed Christian social conscience.

The viable state today has to be resolutely turned towards reform and change. The only sure stability in our time is a dynamic, reforming stability. This is one of the reasons why our times can provide a better soil for the Gospel's sowing than earlier, more static centuries. For Christianity is a dynamic religion, always in movement. Christians are a pilgrim people, a people on the march, sure only of the terminus, ill at ease at all the intermediate points on the journey. "We have not here a lasting city: we look for one that is to come." (*Hebrews* 13 : 14.)

The absolute justice and perfect love of that eternal City which is our terminus is such as to make us chronically dissatisfied with any given measure of justice and love in the earthly city. The Christian can never be a die-hard defender of any political or social or class status quo. Such slogans as "I'm all right, Jack", "We've never had it so good" are intolerable for the Christian. If he is not more concerned about others, especially the dependent and the needy, than about his own status and differentials, then, as St Paul puts it, the Christian has denied the faith and is worse than an unbeliever. (1 *Timothy* 5 : 8.)

I believe that the younger generation are ready for this challenge to reforming change and will rise to it. God's gifts to them of youth, optimism, openness, education and grace, fit them to build the Christian society of the last quarter of the twentieth century.

YOUNG IRELAND
One can meaningfully speak today of a Young Ireland. It is true that one must be sceptical of slogans applying the cheer-words "young" and "new" to nations. The oldest and sickest forms of human degeneracy can be passed off as brave young virtues — as they were by

Nazi and Fascist or Communist propaganda. But there is a true sense in which the future Republic of Ireland will be a younger society, in which the presence of youth will be more significant than it has been in this country for many a generation.

For one thing, emigration has been decisively slowed down, and more young people will stay and work and marry in Ireland. One of the saddest results of emigration in the recent past was that it drained off our youth and with them much of our energy, initiative and zest for progress and change. It left us prone to be a static society, complacent in the security of the status quo, afraid of and resistant to change.

In future, our population in the Republic will become gradually better balanced. The proportion of young to middle-aged and older persons will increase. The place of young people in the shaping of society will become more important also because of their better education and because of their possession of the vote at 18. The first generation of 18-year-olds to exercise the vote will also be, in principle, the best educated phalanx of voters ever to vote in Ireland. This makes the electorate's answer to the second question in the recent referendum one of the most decisive events in Irish political history for many decades.

Doubtless some politicians think the young voters will respond to the same slogans, react to the same Pavlovian stimuli, as those which always worked before. I hope they are wrong. I think they are wrong.

I believe the young voters will be more reflective, more questioning, more impatient for social justice. I hope they will be readier for change. Not all change is good; and some of the changes going on in Irish society are odious. They merely show that Ireland has no inoculation against selfishness, vulgarity, ruthless property dealing, heartless drive for quick profit.

Not all change is good; but without the right sorts of change there can be no moral progress and no just society. Young people brought up in a changing Ireland can help the older among us to discern rightful from harmful change and to accept the commitment to rightful change which is a condition of justice and brotherhood.

I find it impossible to believe that an educated new generation in Ireland will go on living by the tribal myths and unthinking catch-cries which have for so long torn society into closed, suspicious factions in the North, and which have so long paralysed progress in the South. I believe the next generation can build a better Ireland.

From the White Paper to a New Beginning

The White Paper, *Northern Ireland Constitutional Proposals,* awaited with concern by all, with confidence by few, with scepticism or with fear by many, has appeared. No-one's fears have been wholly realised, no-one's scepticism fully justified. No community or group has been completely satisfied; but in the Northern Ireland situation, this can be seen as tribute rather than as criticism. No community or group has been wholly rebuffed either, except those who completely eschew the democratic process of advancing political aims by peaceful discussion and persuasion. The White Paper has been received by the major political groupings responsibly and by the man in the street soberly and seriously. Above all, as at Day Three, the dreaded backlash from either of the militant wings has not materialised; and this is relief enough and reward enough for its hard-working authors and for the anxiously-waiting public.

BRITISH GOVERNMENT POLICY PROGRESS

It can scarcely be denied that the White Paper represents a significant shift in British Government attitudes and policies towards Northern Ireland. After imposing the Partition settlement in Ireland, that Government spent fifty years in the hand-washing ritual of maintaining at one and the same time three contradictory claims: first, that there was no problem in Northern Ireland; second, that if there were problems, they were domestic matters within the exclusive competence of the Stormont Parliament, which could not even be raised at Westminster; third, that there might indeed be problems, but they were exclusively the prerogative of the Westminster Parliament, since Northern Ireland was an integral part of the United Kingdom and no foreign power, especially not the Irish Republic, could interfere.

In the critical years since 1969, British Government indecision and delay have been an important factor in the deteriorating situation. Opportunity after opportunity has been missed. The vacillation and indecision, compounded by the amazing opaqueness and unwisdom of British Army counter-violence policies and tactics, played into the hands of the men of violence on both sides. As the White Paper itself says, in what might be read as a mood of repentance, "Northern Ireland has been the focus of speculation and uncertainty for a prolonged period already, and there can be little doubt that as long as such uncertainty continues to exist, it will be exploited by those who seek to prey upon the fears of the communities". It is to be hoped that the lesson has at last been learnt and that the utmost practicable urgency will be given now to the implementation of the new Constitutional Proposals, and the holding of elections preparatory to setting in place the new structures.

The minority community, to speak only of it, has, by long and sad experience, been rendered so sceptical and even so cynical that they will acquire confidence in the new structures only when they *see* their own representatives really sharing in administration and, above all, in executive power. At the same time, the minority community must show unreserved willingness to co-operate and to participate in making the new structures work. Only in this way can the majority community be convinced that it has no reason either to distrust the minority's commitment to building new structures in peace, or to doubt the minority's ability to make a contribution to public life as valuable as any ever made by a unionist.

TWO COMMUNITIES

One of the most valuable parts of the White Paper and one which marks a significant reappraisal of past British conventions is the unambiguous recognition that in Northern Ireland there are two communities and not just only one; and that democratic structures in Northern Ireland must relate to that peculiar two-community situation. The population of Northern Ireland is consistently referred to as "the communities" in the plural; and these are recognised as having a "clash of national aspirations" and as being divided by "patterns of education, housing and employment; general social attitudes and responses; history, culture and tradition". The irremediable defect of the Stormont experiment is recognised as having been the exclusion of an entire community as community from sharing in power, with the consequent absence of "government by consent". It is acknowledged that "current British constitutional conventions" as applied in Northern Ireland worked in an undemocratic way, because "the same party has been the majority party after each General Election"; and "that party has never returned to Parliament in the course of half a century a member from the minority community which comprises more than a third of the population". The document concludes: "There is no future for devolved institutions of government in Northern Ireland unless majority and minority alike can be bound . . . to the support of new political arrangements". The logic of this thinking is carried into the proposals for the composition of the future Executive: "It is the view of the Government that the Executive itself can no longer be solely based upon any single party, if that party draws its support and its elected representatives virtually entirely from only one section of a divided community".

OATH

The implication of all these paragraphs and of the central thrust of the White Paper is that nationalists and republicans will be invited to participate, alongside of unionists, at all levels of the new governmental structures. After all, the fundamental defect which the present proposals are designed to eradicate was that a Catholic could share in power only if he renounced nationalist aspirations and embraced unionist ones. In the light of this, it is disturbing to read that, although the "oath of allegiance" is abolished for all other posts and offices, an oath is required for members of the Executive. This matter requires clarification. The whole purpose of the new structures will be defeated if the suggested oath requires "allegiance to the Crown", which nationalists and republicans by definition cannot sincerely profess; or if the oath is inconsistent, in the Northern Ireland situation, with what the White Paper itself recognises as a basic human right, namely "freedom to advance any political or constitutional cause by non-violent means". In the same section on human rights, the White Paper makes the latter phrase still more specific, by speaking of "disagreement since the earliest years of Northern Ireland's existence, not just about how Northern Ireland should be governed, but as to whether it should continue to exist at all". The document goes on in that context to say that "any person in Northern Ireland, whatever his political beliefs, may advance them peacefully without fear". The oath required of members of the Executive, if there is to be an oath, must without qualification allow this right to all those who formally and explicitly "seek the unification of Ireland by consent".

DENOMINATIONAL EDUCATION

The studious effort of the White Paper to establish a balanced and fair appraisal of the situation is well exemplified in its section on education. It is gratifying to read the judgment that : "To make the educational system itself the scapegoat for the ills of Northern Ireland would obscure problems whose origins are of a much more complex character." The text goes on, of course, to welcome evidences of the will to cooperation between the State and the Catholic school systems and concludes that "it will be a vital task of government in the future to facilitate, to encourage and to promote these points of contact".

Calls for "desegregated schooling" — to use the fashionable but emotive question-begging term — serve much more to reactivate polemics than to promote reconciliation. The Northern Catholic community has made great sacrifices, for reasons of conscience and religious conviction, to preserve their Catholic schools. Proposals to remove the Catholic character of these schools could only be seen by them as one further threat of repressive and discriminatory action, one more attempt to damage them as a community.

HUMAN RIGHTS

Part 4 of the White Paper, entitled "A Charter of Human Rights", although it betrays at several points a nervous preoccupation with giving everyone something to please them, has, nevertheless, some admirable statements of principle and of intent. Indeed, in some respects, this section marks the most important change in historic British attitudes towards Ireland and offers the greatest hope of a just and peaceful future. As already stated, this section promises full civic rights and full political equality to all citizens and groups, whether their ambition be to preserve a "British Ulster" or to promote a United Ireland — the only condition being that they "seek to advance their views by peaceful democratic means alone". The section also contains repeated and firm assurances of the complete outlawing of discriminatory practices of all kinds, whether in public employment, in the public or private sectors of industry, or in housing and civil benefits.

AMBIGUITIES AND INADEQUACIES

At a number of crucial and critical points it must be concluded that the White Paper loses nerve and runs away from real problems into ambiguity or near-equivocation. One of these issues is the vital question of the police force. Both the prevailing violence and the breakdown both of law observance and of respect for law and for the agencies of law-enforcement make the question of a re-constituted police service one of the most fundamental importance for the restoration of normal social life in the North. It will take very much more than the anaemic phrases of the White Paper to provide a police force which, for the first time in the history of the State, will command the confidence and the respect of both communities and of all age-groups in the Six Counties. This is one of the weakest sections in the whole White Paper, although the problem is a central one for the achievement of the document's stated purpose of "winning that wide-ranging consent upon which the government of a free country must rest".

Another grave weakness of these Constitutional Proposals is the treatment of the much-trumpeted Irish

Dimension. It is not entirely convincing for the drafters to argue that the Council of Ireland can be set up and can operate only "with the consent of both majority and minority opinion in Northern Ireland, who have a right to prior consultation and involvement in the process of determining its form, functions and procedures".

This vagueness and indecisiveness coheres badly with the White Paper's recognition that the immediate causes of the North's tragedy are, on the one hand, the absence of "government by consent", and on the other, the campaign of violence on behalf of a fraction of the non-consenting community. This non-consenting community is, by the White Paper's own confession, committed to Irish nationalism and to the achievement of Irish unity on a basis of consent. This being so, the non-consenting community, which is now being invited to consent, is being expected to do so without having built into the new structures any formal structural expression of what is an integral part of its aspiration— to belong ultimately politically, as it already feels it belongs culturally and historically, to an All-Ireland community.

But these and other ambiguities and inadequacies of the White Paper are no justification for refusal to participate. The re-structuring of the police service and the development of a meaningful Council of Ireland are by no means excluded by the document. Its ambiguous language is capable of a "strong" or of a "weak" interpretation on these and on other issues. It is the duty as it is the opportunity of the nationally-minded community to get in on the processes of hermeneutics and to ensure that those interpretations which they believe to be just and right should prevail. This is what politics is about. It is also what peace and justice and democracy are about. It is what civilised society is about.

It would be a strange sign of doubt about the validity of nationalist and republican aspirations to despair of their power to carry conviction by persuasion to those not born into them. Indeed, the most effective way in present conditions of working to make the noble ideal of a reunited Ireland a reality would surely be to "play a truly constructive part" in the "achievement on a constitutional basis of peace, equality and prosperity".

THE EUROPEAN DIMENSION

The Constitutional Proposals are written in the emerging light of a new European future for both Britain and the two parts of Ireland. The significance of our joint entry into the European Economic Community is not indeed developed at length; but clearly it offers an historical opportunity for a really new beginning in the relationships of these islands to one another. There is an enigmatic sentence in the White Paper which says : "It would require either exceptional vision or exceptional fool-hardiness to forecast the future development of relationships involving North and South in Ireland, the United Kingdom and the British Isles and Europe". The challenge to Irish nationalism, in the Republic as well as in the North at the present time, is to strive that the new context of European partnership will give Ireland at last her chance of achieving the aspiration of generations for an Ireland united in tolerance and reconciliation, justice and peace. Surely, if both the Republic and Northern Ireland, both Ireland and Britain, can together belong to a United Europe, it is in the long run irrational for North and South in this island not to come together to form a United Ireland, united by conviction and consent.

THE RELIGIOUS DIMENSION

To stress, as we have done throughout, the responsibility

of politicians is not to deny the responsibilities of Churchmen. We have all failed in the past to make a Christian judgment of the state of our society and to address a Christian judgment to the pre-Christian or post-Christian attitudes competing with Christian values in our own Church communities. In a country where ecumenism is vital to our good name as Irishmen, to our credibility as Christians, to our missionary work abroad, to our collective well-being and even ultimately to our survival as a democratic society, we lag lamentably behind in the ecumenical field.

We must now plan for the vigorous pursuit of ecumenism at every level. The first requirement of ecumenism, according to the Vatican Council, is "every effort to eliminate words, judgments and actions which do not respond to the condition of separated brethren with truth and fairness and so make mutual relations between them more difficult". All Irish Christians should see any harping, from either side, on a polemical past as offence against the ecumenical imperative of the present and the future. We should recall the past with repentance, not recrimination; incidents being recalled, if at all, in sorrow by those who caused suffering, rather than in anger by those who suffered. "Carry each other's troubles", St Paul says, "and fulfil the law of Christ." "Rejoice with those who rejoice," he says elsewhere, "and be sad with those in sorrow." We must, in each community, learn to feel as the other community feels; to suffer when they suffer, as if it were we ourselves who suffered; to rejoice when they rejoice, as if we ourselves had cause to celebrate.

The darkness and devastation of today can be the prelude to an Easter Dawn, which, like the Resurrection itself, can strike us dumb with amazement. So it has been for war-devastated West Germany, which upon its ruins has been able to build both a commitment to peace and an achievement of peace with its neighbours, and a degree of reconciliation and harmony within its frontiers, which it had not known for centuries. From out of the suffering and the rubble of Northern streets we can, all of us, today adapt for our own condition the prayer of Father Erich Przywara in the bomb craters of Munich in 1944 :

O God, we do not understand where your love has gone; we do not understand where our own love has disappeared. All that we experience, all that we know, all that we see, is nothing but devastation, ruin, dust and ashes. All that we feel is the shame in which we lie helpless . . . . And yet we hear your word : "I am the Resurrection and the Life. He who believes in me will not die, but I will raise him up to eternal life". This is your word, Lord. Pronounce it again over our ashes. Say it again over our corruption. Repeat it again in power over our failures. Amen.

Notes

and Index

Notes

[1] English CTS translation p. 46. The last sentence is translated by the author from the original Latin, since the current English translation is defective.

[2] *Church and Colonialism* (Sheed and Ward 1969), p. 110.

[3] *ibid.,* p. 34.

[4] Reported in *The Tablet,* 6 November 1971, pp. 1084-5.

[5] *Contemplation in a World of Action* George Allen and Unwin, 1971, p. 146.

[6] *Strength to Love* Fontana Books, Collins, London (1964), 1972, pp. 14-15.

[7] *The Future of Northern Ireland,* a paper for Discussion, Northern Ireland Office, HMSO 1972.

[8] *Contemplation in a world of Action* George Allen and Unwin, London, 1971, p. XX.

Index